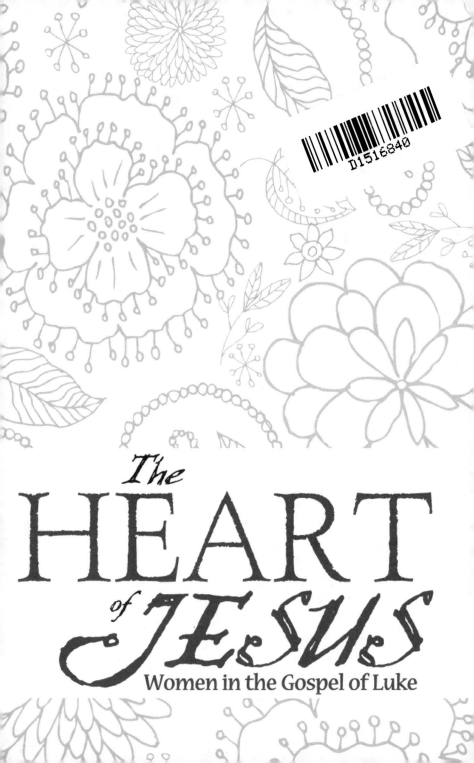

The HEART of JESUS

Women in the Gospel of Luke

Published by Concordia Publishing House
3558 S. Jefferson Ave., St. Louis, MO 63118-3968
1-800-325-3040 · www.cph.org

Table of Contents

INTRODUCTION

Introduction

Christ's coming to earth brought new life, sure hope and great joy to all believers—women included!

Although first century Judaism was much more supportive of women than most of the rest of the world, it was nevertheless what we would consider a chauvinistic society. Women were protected but without rights; respected but without autonomy.

Then Christ came, and the Light of the World turned the light on for women!

In a culture where women were not sent to school, Jesus encouraged them to learn. He included them in His special circle of followers—something totally unheard of at that time. He treated women with courtesy and respect, regardless of their social status, former sinful lifestyle, background, or place of residence. He touched them to heal them, and they touched Him, an act that, in the case of the woman with the flow of blood, made Him ritually unclean. Motivated by their need, He did some of those healings on the Sabbath, a practice that endangered His life. He honored mothers by providing for His own and performing the first recorded miracle in response to her request.

Jesus cared about widows, who often faced a life of poverty, and He restored the life of son of the Widow of Nain without her even asking. He prevented abuse of women and had compassion on one who was crippled. Before healing her, He brought her to the front of the synagogue, even though women were required to stay in the back.

Jesus spoke to women in public, and after His resurrection, He chose a woman, Mary Magdalene, to go and tell the others that He was alive! Women were the first to see Him after He rose from the dead, the first to touch Him, and the first to be commissioned as evangelists of this glorious news.

In His heart, words and actions, Jesus accepted, affirmed, encouraged, and elevated women as partners in sharing the Gospel and serving in His Name. Nowhere does this come through more clearly than in the Gospel of Luke where almost every incident or parable involving a man is balanced with one about a woman.

In The Heart of Jesus, we look at women in Luke's Gospel to discover more about Jesus—to learn how He views us today, how He wants to relate to us, how He encourages and enables us to become all that He created us to be.

But this book does more than talk about Jesus and women—it delves into the background of Biblical women to understand what life was like for them. How did they live? How did they worship? What was it like for Elizabeth to be barren and then have a baby in her senior years? For Mary to become miraculously pregnant out of wedlock? For Anna to spend day and night in the Temple, waiting to see the Savior? For women to be healed, to have children restored to life, to accompany Jesus as He taught, to watch Him die an excruciating death, and then to be the first to see Him alive again?

What was it like to "go and tell" such marvelous news? That's a directive that Christ gives to women (and men) today too, one for which He sends His Holy Spirit as our enabler.

What does this mean for us? To help and motivate us, The Heart of Jesus provides ideas for parenting, mentoring, dealing with loss, advocating for people with disabilities, sharing the Gospel in our community, and serving those in need in the name of our compassionate, forgiving, loving, amazing Lord and Savior!

May you be blessed and encouraged as you read it!

—Marlys Taege Moberg

Chapter ONE

Elizabeth

Family Member, Friend, and Mentor
Luke 1:5–7, 39–45, 56–66

And [Elizabeth and Zechariah] were both righteous before God, walking blamelessly in all the commandments and statutes of the Lord. But they had no child, because Elizabeth was barren, and both were advanced in years. Luke 1:6–7

[Elizabeth to Mary:] "Blessed are you among women, and blessed is the fruit of your womb! And why is this granted to me that the mother of my Lord should come to me? For behold, when the sound of your greeting came to my ears, the baby in my womb leaped for joy." Luke 1:42–44

My son-in-law, Marshall, was born on my wedding day. Whenever I think of this, I marvel at how intimately God is at work in our lives. As I walked down the aisle to pledge my love to my waiting groom, the Lord was already providing a husband for our daughter Lauren, who would not even be conceived for more than two years.

In college, Lauren met a young man named John, and they became engaged. His father was a highly respected Christian doctor whose specialty was developmental disabilities. By that time, I was working at Bethesda Lutheran Home in Watertown, Wisconsin, a residential training and care center for more than six hundred people with mental and physical disabilities. We were seeking a staff doctor.

After learning of the need through Lauren's connection with their family, John's father became Bethesda's first full-time medical director, a position he filled admirably until his retirement and with great benefit to the residents. About the time he accepted Bethesda's job offer, Lauren and John broke their engagement, and each went on to eventually marry someone else. In Lauren's case, Marshall.

Although we may not recognize it at first when God is at work, His timing is always perfect and His will is accomplished. Through all the events of life, His purpose is ultimately and always achieved. The Creator's action in the life of Elizabeth gives us a picture of that perfect planning.

The Calamity of Childlessness

Elizabeth's life beautifully demonstrates our Lord's intimate love and care, but that care wasn't always so apparent early in her marriage. In those days, most women's sphere of influence was limited to the home. A woman's primary vocations were wife and mother. Children were then, just as they are today, a blessing of God (Genesis 49:25, Deuteronomy 30:9). God "opened the womb" so a woman could conceive (Genesis 29:31). Because barrenness could result as a consequence of sin, childlessness carried a stigma, regardless of the circumstances (compare Leviticus 20:20–21; Deuteronomy 28:15, 18). Bearing children was so critical to maintaining the family heritage that barren wives like Sarah and, later, Rachel (Genesis 16:1–16; 30:3–7) gave their maidservants to their husbands in order to conceive an heir. As Rachel said to Jacob, "Give me children, or I shall die!" (Genesis 30:1).

With all that in mind, imagine Elizabeth's sorrow over the years. Both she and her husband, Zechariah, were members of the tribe of Levi, the tribe charged by God to lead His people in matters of faith. She was the daughter of a priest, and her husband was a priest. Moreover, both were "righteous before God, walking blamelessly in all the commandments and statutes of the Lord" (Luke 1:6). Through their early years together, they must have held hopes for God's blessing. But as the years passed and they remained childless, they may have begun to wonder if the Lord might be punishing them instead.

How easily God's children forget that God's timing is not our timing. The apostle Peter reminds us, "With the Lord one day is as a thousand years, and a thousand years as one day" (2 Peter 3:8). When days lengthen into years, we can rest on God's promise: "In the time of my favor I will answer you" (Isaiah 49:8 NIV).

When Luke introduces us to Zechariah and Elizabeth, they are senior citizens, "advanced in years" (Luke 1:7). In light of their long wait for "the time of [His] favor," it's interesting to note that *Zechariah* means "Yahweh remembers," while *Elizabeth* means "the oath of God." They are about to learn that God has chosen them for a high honor indeed! Their son, the son of their old age, will be the forerunner of His Son.

Both Zechariah and Elizabeth descended from Aaron, the priestly division of the tribe of Levi. God charged Aaron and the priests who followed him with teaching the people His will and law. They were also to be mediators, interceding for the people:

> *Aaron was set apart to dedicate the most holy things, that he and his sons forever should make offerings before the LORD and minister to Him and pronounce blessings in His name forever.*
> *1 Chronicles 23:13*

When Israel took possession of the Promised Land, the other eleven tribes received parcels of land as their inheritance. The tribe of Levi received no land. Instead, the Lord Himself was their inheritance (Deuteronomy 18:1; Joshua 13:14; 18:19–24). They received tithes of the produce and cattle the other Israelites brought to the Lord, and they also relied on the offerings (bulls, goats, lambs, doves, pigeons, and grain) brought to the central sanctuary in worship. The Levites also received forty-eight towns with pasturelands scattered throughout the land; thirteen of these towns were set aside specifically for Aaron's descendants. This made it possible for many Levites to live among the other eleven tribes, teaching the Scriptures and resolving disputes that arose. This explains why Zechariah and Elizabeth lived in the "hill country" of Judah (Luke 1:39).

At the time of King David, the tribe of Levi included thirty-eight thousand men (1 Chronicles 23:3). David organized the tribe, assigning each family a specific role. The descendants of Aaron served as priests; the other Levites assisted the priests. They also served as singers, musicians, and preparers of the holy oils used in worship. They gathered wood and took care of the shewbread (cakes or loaves offered to God and always present in the temple). They became gatekeepers, guards, keepers of the treasury, and cleaners of the temple (1 Chronicles 23).[1]

The priests, all descended from Aaron, were divided into twenty-four groups, taking turns serving in the temple, week by week. Each group thus served only one week in twenty-four. All of the priests shared duties during the four weeks in which the nation celebrated the major festivals.

The details of the nation's worship had not always been so formalized. Early in the history of God's chosen people, it focused on sacrifices offered on outdoor altars. Then came more formal worship in the tabernacle (a portable tent) in the wilderness. Solomon built the first temple in Jerusalem. The Babylonian army destroyed it and carried the Jewish people into captivity in Babylon in 587 BC. There, the people worshiped in synagogues. When God brought His people home to Jerusalem in 538 BC, Zerubbabel led construction of a second temple.

Sacrifices were a primary focus of worship at the tabernacle and both temples, but they were never a feature of synagogue worship. In the synagogues, the people prayed, confessed their belief in the one true God, and received the Lord's blessing. The synagogue leader—or sometimes, a guest speaker—would read from Old Testament scrolls and then explain the meaning of the day's text while sitting up front, in the "Seat of Moses." Then the people discussed what the passage of the day meant for them at that time. Men sat in the front and women at the back (or in the balcony in larger synagogues).

While Zechariah's division was taking its turn at the temple, he was chosen by lot to burn incense on the altar designated especially for that purpose. This was a very special honor that normally happened only *once in a lifetime*. He must have thought again and again of how pleased and joyous Elizabeth would be when he told her!

Incense was burned twice a day, morning and night, on the altar located in the Holy Place, just in front of the curtain that separated the Holy Place from the Holy of Holies. Incense consisted of a mixture of perfumes, spices (gum resin and aromatic mollusk shells), frankincense, and salt, all ground into a powder. It was treated as holy and never used by individuals for personal purposes (Exodus 30:34–38).

While the incense burned, the crowd of worshipers prayed outside in the temple court. The smoke of the incense pictured the prayers of God's people ascending heavenward. It may also have served a secondary purpose of masking the odors of the burning flesh of sacrifices on the huge main altar. The bronze altar in Solomon's temple was thirty feet square and fifteen feet high (2 Chronicles 4:1).

For four hundred years there had been only silence from the Lord. Not since the days of Malachi, Ezra, Haggai, and Nehemiah had the Israelites received a prophetic message. Although the Jews had prayed often for the promised Messiah to come, it is unlikely that anyone expected an answer on this particular day. After all, Zechariah, not the high priest, was on duty. A simple, rugged man from a rural town, he was not part of the Jerusalem elite.

Moreover, the second temple was undergoing remodeling by King Herod. This building, constructed by Zerubbabel, in no way compared with Solomon's temple. Herod's goal was to enlarge both the site and the building, to "bring it to perfection." Seeking to gain popularity with the Jews, he wanted the bigger and better structure to be the "most glorious of all his actions."[2]

In the midst of this reconstruction, which began about 19 BC and took more than eighty years to complete, the angel brought startling news to the elderly Zechariah. The aged man and his wife would have a son, who was to be named John (meaning "God is gracious"). It's a wonder the priest (and later, the postmenopausal Elizabeth) didn't laugh in unbelief like Sarah. Their son was to be a Nazirite, dedicated to the Lord like Samson. Nazirites never drank fermented beverages or cut their hair, and they avoided corpses and graves. The angel also gave Zechariah this reassurance: "You will have joy and gladness, and many will rejoice at his birth, for he will be great before the Lord" (Luke 1:14–15).

The angel also said he would be "filled with the Holy Spirit, even from his mother's womb. And he will turn many of the children of Israel to the Lord their God, and he will go before [the Messiah] in the spirit and power of Elijah, to turn the hearts of the fathers to the children, and the disobedient to the wisdom of the just" (Luke 1:15b–17).

Wow! That was more than Zechariah could believe! Wondering if he was dreaming, he reminded Gabriel of how old he and Elizabeth were. A baby was almost impossible at their age! "How can I be sure of this?" he asked. Yet, Zechariah's unbelief couldn't stop God's holy purpose. Neither can our own lack of faith derail God's purposes of love in our lives.

Zechariah forgot, as we often do, too, that with God, nothing is impossible. Because of his unbelief, Zechariah lost his ability to speak until his son was born. How would he deal with it? How would *we* react if our husband lost his voice for nine months, especially when he'd had an amazing experience? We'd want to hear every last detail!

Apparently Zechariah did manage to communicate by signing and writing. What would he have used for his messages? For permanent manuscripts, clay tablets, papyrus, and expensive parchment were used. More likely, Zechariah used the same implements schoolboys used: small, wax-coated wooden tablets with a pointed stylus made of metal or bone. One end of the stylus was blunt for erasures and the other, sharp for writing.

When his time of service in the temple was completed, Zechariah returned home, and soon, just as the angel had said, Elizabeth became pregnant.

Nevertheless, the happy couple waited to share their good news. They were past the normal years of childbearing. A premature announcement could bring on unwelcome laughter and gossip from family and friends. Perhaps for other reasons, too, Elizabeth remained in seclusion for five months. Was she troubled with morning sickness? Was she caring for Zechariah, who might not have wanted to venture out in his speechless condition? Did she simply need extra rest because of her age? (Some Bible scholars think she was at least sixty years old, possibly seventy or more. Scripture does not tell us.) Perhaps in the early months, Elizabeth did not want to face the ridicule and pity of her neighbors who may have thought her delusional to believe she was expecting a baby so late in life.

We cannot know, but whatever the case, Elizabeth demonstrated her faith during this time by praising God and exclaiming, "How kind the Lord is! ... He has taken away my disgrace of having no children" (Luke 1:25 NLT). It would have been so easy for her initially to doubt Gabriel's message, as Zechariah had. Instead, she trusted and acknowledged: "The Lord done this for me" (Luke 1:25 NIV).

Noting the various translations of Luke 1:25 gives us a deeper understanding of what Elizabeth endured in her childlessness. She praised God who took away "my reproach among men" (KJV), "my shame among the people" (NIRV), and "my disgrace" (NLT). Now at last she could rejoice!

No doubt her happiness increased when Mary came to visit. During the sixth month of Elizabeth's pregnancy, the angel Gabriel made another appearance, this time to a younger woman, with an even more amazing piece of news. Mary, a virgin, was to become the mother of the Son of God! The angel's message included the fact that Elizabeth also was expecting a child.

Despite her thrilled acceptance of her new role, Mary was just a teenager with many questions and no experience in mothering. In that society, girls could be married as young as age 12, but most were probably 15 or 16.[3] A girl's immediate family could ostracize her if the baby in her womb was not fathered by her betrothed, and Joseph could legally have had her stoned to death. Stoning was not uncommon in those days. Yes, in time, the angel did inform Joseph, but no angel spoke to her parents or the rest of the family. We can imagine that many people would have gossiped about the "story Mary cooked up" to cover her immorality!

Mentoring Needed

Mary must have been bursting to discuss all this with someone who would understand, someone who could advise and encourage and rejoice with her. Elizabeth, with the wisdom of years and also miraculously expecting for the first time, was a logical mentor.

Mary quickly prepared and hurried to Elizabeth's

home. Scholars believe that Zechariah and Elizabeth lived in Hebron, the only city given to the tribe of Levi in Judea. Hebron was twenty-five miles south of Jerusalem and about one hundred miles from Nazareth, where Mary lived—a journey of three to five days.

How did she travel? We don't know. Most people walked. Some rode donkeys. It would have been unsafe for her to travel alone, so she may have joined a caravan journeying in the same direction. Today we don't arrive for a three-month visit unannounced, but in Bible times (before the advent of the telephone, E-mail capabilities, or even postal service), relatives and other visitors were usually welcomed whenever they arrived. Family mattered, and extra space would always be found for anyone related by blood.

For Elizabeth at this time, Mary's arrival would have been an unexpected blessing. Filled with the Holy Spirit, Elizabeth felt the baby in her womb joyously leap in greeting and recognition of the presence of the unborn Son of God. In a loud voice she exclaimed: "Blessed are you among women and blessed is the child you will bear! But why am I so favored that the mother of my Lord should come to me?" (Luke 1:42–43 NIV).

Feeling the movement of an unborn child is always so exciting and reassuring during pregnancy, but the baby's leap had even deeper meaning. It indicated not only the life of her own baby, but the presence of the long-awaited Savior Himself in Mary's womb! For Mary, Elizabeth's exclamation was the first recognition, the first confession by another human being, that her baby was the Son of God! What a reassurance Elizabeth's words must have provided for the pregnant virgin!

Here was a relative (either a cousin or an aunt; translations vary), a family member who understood. Here was another mother-to-be who also recognized and rejoiced in the miracle that was occurring and who trusted the message of the angel. Here was a friend with whom she could discuss the changes taking place in her body, the forthcoming birth process, how to deal with the comments and advice of neighbors, as well as all the doubts and uncertainties human beings encounter as they face an unknown and unexpected God-ordained future.

Scripture encourages older women to teach younger women (Titus 2:3–5). As the devout wife of a priest and an older member of the tribe entrusted with sharing God's Word, Elizabeth was well prepared to mentor Mary. Certainly Mary's trust in the Lord was an encouragement to Elizabeth too.

Mary's visit lasted three months. Scripture gives no indication as to whether she returned home before or after Elizabeth gave birth to John. Maybe she left before the baby came to give Elizabeth more peace and privacy. Maybe she stayed until afterward to assist with the birth and be better prepared through personal experience for what lay ahead of her.

Whatever the case, her time in Judea was undoubtedly a blessing for both women. How Mary and Elizabeth must have talked and listened and shared and rejoiced and wondered about the miracles taking place. At last Elizabeth would have a baby, a son who would be "great before the Lord," who would "be filled with the Holy Spirit, even from his mother's womb," who would have the "spirit and power of Elijah," and who would bring many people back to God (Luke 1:15–17). And at last, the long-expected Savior would be born!

How much we, like Elizabeth and Mary, need companionship and understanding as we face unanticipated challenges in life, even when they bring unexpected blessings. We need someone to listen, to react, to comfort and encourage us. We all need a home and family circle that provides a safe place where we are accepted for who God made us to be. In many cultures, close-knit families have met that need. In centuries past (and in some cultures today), people lived their entire life in the same community, often with three generations in the same house.

When I was a child, it was common for relatives to just drop in for a visit. Sunday afternoons especially were a time for going to Grandma's house or stopping at the home of a relative or neighbor. Today, with many living in gated communities or high-rise apartments and condos, visits are infrequent and scheduled. Even children make play dates. Maintaining close relationships with relatives scattered around the globe is often difficult. We may not see some family members for years. In such situations, it's important to make a special effort to remain in touch. Fortunately, paper is cheap, readily available, and easily mailed, unlike the expensive parchment of ancient times or the clumsiness of wax and clay tablets. Even better, we have the blessing of phones and E-mail. Whether our children, siblings, or parents are in Europe, Africa, India, or the Middle East, we can hear their voices, learn of their needs, and rejoice in their successes.

Although people in Bible times lacked the advantages of communication and transportation we enjoy, relatives and neighbors were usually involved at every stage of life. When Elizabeth's son was born, Luke reports, her neighbors and relatives "rejoiced with her," and "on the eighth day they came to circumcise the child" (Luke 1:58–59).

A healthy delivery to an older woman would have been cause for celebration indeed.

In the ceremony of circumcision, a flint knife was used to cut off the foreskin of a male's penis. As the American Bible Society Web site explains, "Circumcision is first mentioned in the Bible in connection with God's promise to make Abraham's descendants a great nation and to give them a land they could call their own. In return, Abraham and his descendants were to obey God. To show that they were keeping their promise to God, every male descendant of Abraham was to be circumcised (Genesis 17:1–14)."[4] For Jews at the time of Christ, circumcision carried as deep a significance as Baptism carries for Christians today.

In Jesus Christ, God's covenant with Abraham was fulfilled. In Christ's cross, our sins are forgiven. We are incorporated into the family of God by Baptism. Paul writes in Colossians: "In Him you were also circumcised, in the putting off of the sinful nature, not with a circumcision done by the hands of men but with the circumcision done by Christ, having been buried with Him in baptism and raised with Him through your faith in the power of God, who raised Him from the dead" (2:11–12 NIV).

His Name Is John

Had they followed the custom of the day, Zechariah and Elizabeth would have named their first son after his father. All the neighbors assumed the baby would be called "Zechariah." To their surprise, Elizabeth spoke up: "No; he shall be called John" (Luke 1:60). Obviously, Zechariah had communicated the angel's message in detail to Elizabeth via his wax tablet. Obviously, too, Elizabeth believed her pregnancy was an amazing miracle as foretold by the angel, and not an accident or an anomaly.

The relatives persisted: "None of your relatives is called by this name" (v. 61). Not believing Elizabeth, they looked at the father and "made signs to [him]" (v. 62). But Zechariah wasn't deaf! They didn't need to make signs to him.

In response, Zechariah asked for his tablet. In affirmation of Elizabeth and to everyone's astonishment, he wrote, "His name is John." Immediately, the priest could talk! Filled with the Holy Spirit, he began praising God and prophesying. The Redeemer was on His way! He would deliver His people from their enemies (v. 74). And Zechariah and Elizabeth would experience special, personal joy:

> *And you, child, will be called the prophet of the Most High; for you will go before the Lord to prepare His ways, to give knowledge of salvation to His people in the forgiveness of their sins, because of the tender mercy of our God, whereby the sunrise shall visit us from on high to give light to those who sit in darkness and in the shadow of death, to guide our feet into the way of peace. Luke 1:76–79*

The word spread quickly; soon everyone throughout the hill country of Judea was talking about this amazing event. The Savior King was coming. His forerunner was already here!

God gives His faith-filled women today the same privilege He gave Elizabeth—that of responding to God with complete trust in His Word, faith in His promises, patience in view of His timing, and praise for His blessings. Like Elizabeth, we are called to be caring family members, good friends, and helpful mentors. And like her, we do this as our Lord, by His Spirit, empowers us.

Family and *mentor* are old words that have taken on expanded meanings today. *Family* in the Old Testament usually means people related by birth, adoption, or marriage. In Genesis 7:1, God told Noah, "Go into the ark, you and all your household, for I have seen that you are righteous in this generation." In Genesis 46:27, seventy members of Jacob's family went to Egypt. In the wilderness (Numbers 2:2), the Israelites had to "camp each by his own standard, with the banners of their fathers' houses. They shall camp facing the tent of meeting on every side." Because of Joshua's promise to Rahab, her entire family was saved when Jericho was destroyed by the Israelites (Joshua 6:23). Some families, like that of Izrahiah, were very large (1 Chronicles 7:4 NIV): "According to their family genealogy, they had 36,000 men ready for battle, for they had many wives and sons."

The scriptural use of the word *family* clearly indicates the human, biological, adoptive, and spiritual definition. Today, however, "family" applies to many different situations. We recognize the "nuclear family," consisting of parents and children. But "family" can also be used to describe students living in the same college dorm, employees in a work group, or residents in a senior living community. It may include radio personalities who "talk with us" as we drive, TV stars who "come into our homes" on a nightly basis, and members of Armed Forces units who grow closer than brothers and sisters as together they endure battlefield hardships and dangers.

"Family" may also include people we don't know personally. For example, when Rick and Carol Bernstein raised more vegetables than they needed in their Maryland home garden, they took the extras to a homeless mission. Although Rick made many trips with garden donations, he felt something was missing from his acts of generosity—God! Deciding to read through the Bible in its entirety, he was struck by Christ's statement that "as you did it to one of the least of these My brothers, you did it to Me" (Matthew 25:40).

In the process, God led Rick to become a Christian, and his life took on a whole new meaning. Feeling the need to do more for the members of his homeless "family," Rick and Carol bought a two-hundred-acre farm. When his new neighbors learned what the novice farmer was doing, they willingly became mentors. He received additional advice from leaders of the Maryland Food Bank and the Mid-Atlantic Gleaning Network. With the help of church members, youth groups, and adult volunteers, over a million pounds of fresh produce was harvested and given away between 2004 and 2007.[5]

"Family" can also include friends from the past. A woman I had not seen for more than thirty years approached me at a recent Christian women's conference. She and her husband had moved to Arkansas when his health declined after retirement. When he died, she returned to Milwaukee to "be near family." She explained, "My daughter is in New York, one son is in North Wisconsin, and the other is in Arkansas! Nevertheless, I have family here—my church and my friends!"

That fits what we see in the New Testament, which adds a significant dimension to the word. Galatians 6:10 urges us, "Let us do good to everyone, and especially to those who are of the household of faith." In Ephesians 3:14–15, Paul states, "For this reason I bow my knees before the Father, from whom every family in heaven and on earth is named." Hebrews 2:11 tells us, "He who sanctifies and those who are sanctified all have one source. That is why [Jesus] is not ashamed to call them brothers."

Through the waters of Baptism, all believers have become part of the family of God! We are brothers and sisters of Christ. We are sons and daughters of the King—princes and princesses!

As members of the royal family, we have important responsibilities. We need to "be there" for our church members and other Christians when they are hurting or in need. God expects us to pray with and for them, to listen, to sympathize, to encourage, to care, to provide, to offer hospitality just as Elizabeth welcomed Mary . . . to treat them as family.

About ten years ago, my husband was sent to the Gaza Strip for a month to teach an intensive introductory sociology course to thirty-five students seeking a college degree in various disability services. (Audiologists, speech therapists, and other healthcare professionals were especially needed there because of numerous disabilities resulting from intermarriage with close relatives and from conflict injuries in Gaza.)

While there, he participated in a Christian Bible class. Noticing one of his students in attendance and seeing him struggle to read the Bible in English (a second language for him), my husband offered to get him an English-Arabic Bible so he could read it in his "heart" language. The young man declined: "No, because then my parents would know what I was reading." His parents were Muslim, and they could murder him for leaving the family religion. Today, religiously divided families present a new challenge for us as mentors in the United States, where diversity of religions and cultures is rapidly increasing.

In years gone by, the term *mentor* evoked pictures of a learned man in a Roman toga counseling younger men. Today mentoring has gone modern. Mentors no longer need a toga or a title. Nor is mentoring restricted to men, as Elizabeth demonstrated.

Scripture identifies other female mentors. The wise woman of Abel (2 Samuel 20:18–22) mentored Sheba and the residents of Abel, thus saving her city and keeping the peace. Timothy's mother and grandmother, Eunice and Lois, shared their faith with him (2 Timothy 1:5). In Titus 2:3–5, older women are urged to be an example to younger women, training them to be a good example of the Christian faith. Priscilla and Aquila mentored Apollos, a zealous missionary.

How are women doing it today? Their mentoring reaches beyond their nuclear families. A 2006 survey of Lutheran Women's Missionary League (LWML) leaders in South Wisconsin discovered these examples:[6]

- *One woman who works with confirmands, described her role as "loving, caring, encouraging, helping, agreeing and disagreeing, spending time with them, and crying and laughing with them." Sometimes the tables are turned as teenagers teach parents and grandparents to master the Internet and computers or as young women with business experience help other women break the "glass ceiling" on the job.*

- *"Mentoring is helping someone develop an unutilized God-given talent," said another survey respondent. "It means allowing them to fail and then helping them grow from that failure. Too many times we just do something for someone to make sure it gets done correctly and on time. Sometimes mentoring is hard work because you have to nudge and encourage and then nudge and encourage some more, even when you know it would be so much easier just to do it yourself."*

- *"A mentor is not a boss, but a friend," added a third respondent. "Walking alongside, a mentor gently coaches when the need arises. She does not unload all [she knows] at one time and then sit back. She is available and makes contact when she hasn't heard from her 'mentee' recently."*

- *"Mentors recognize your interest in something, then water you like a plant so you develop and grow in your interest," said a fourth woman. "They supply you with resources, materials and suggestions, advice and praise. They listen. They are patient. And, who knows, they might even love you!"*

Elizabeth undoubtedly loved Mary. The older woman exercised the gift of hospitality and modeled trust and love in her Lord. Family mattered to her. So strong was her example that after the circumcision of her newborn son and the return of her husband's voice, "The neighbors were all filled with awe, and throughout the hill country of Judea people were talking about all these things" (Luke 1:65 NIV).

We may not realize every one of our hopes and dreams, but, like Elizabeth, we can nonetheless find comfort and joy by trusting in God's promise of forgiveness and salvation. We may find ourselves surprised by the turn of events in our lives, but no matter where life takes us, we can be sure that our heavenly Father treasures each one of us as His precious daughters, sisters of His Son. He cares about our earthly cares and gives us life forever through faith in Jesus. His presence is sure; therefore, we can be sure we are forever secure.

When the circumstances of life cause us to doubt, we can encourage one another in the Lord who blessed and kept Elizabeth. When our circumstances catch us off guard, we can remind one another to remember all God did for Mary. God came to each of these women in His perfect time in His perfect way, to help and strengthen. And God comes to each of us as well—in His Word and in His Holy Supper. By the power of His Holy Spirit, our hearts leap for joy!

May our trust in our Savior, our sharing of the Good News, the example we set in our families, and our concern for the needs of the hurting people around us fill our towns, cities, and neighborhoods with awe. And may many come to Christ through our words and deeds of witness.

The Heart of Jesus as Shown in Elizabeth's Life

Our all-powerful and merciful triune God, who created the earth, loves us and works through us so that His will is accomplished in His time and His way for the ultimate benefit of all.

Chapter TWO

Mary

Mother of Our Lord, Dedicated Parent
Luke 1:26–38, 46–55; 2:1–52; 8:19–21; 11:27–28

The angel said to her, "Do not be afraid, Mary, for you have found favor with God. And behold, you will conceive in your womb and bear a son, and you shall call His name Jesus. He will be great and will be called the Son of the Most High. The Lord God will give to Him the throne of His father David, and He will reign over the house of Jacob forever, and of His kingdom there will be no end."

Luke 1:30–33

A highlight of the year at Bethesda Lutheran Home is always the Christmas program presented by the residents early in December. One year, several of the cast members, including Mary, were in wheelchairs. As Mary and Joseph approached the elderly innkeeper, seeking a place to stay, he surveyed the scene with frustration and then gave an unscripted answer: "No room! No room! Too many wheelchairs!"

In Bible times, there was no room in the Bethlehem inn either. The city was crowded because many people, like Mary and Joseph, had traveled to Bethlehem when Caesar Augustus ordered a census of the entire Roman world. Every man had to return to his city of origin to register.

Since the main purpose for the census was taxation, some theologians believe Joseph may have owned property in Bethlehem, as these taxes were based on property. Some scholars have noted that pottery samples suggest a migration of people from Bethlehem to Nazareth early in the first century. Perhaps Joseph had grown up in Bethlehem and it remained his legal residence.[7]

A bigger mystery, though, revolves around the question of why Joseph took Mary with him when the baby was due at any time. That was a long walk—or a long ride on the back of a donkey—and it was only males who had to register. Was there no one to befriend Mary in Nazareth because of her questionable pregnancy? To believers, the obvious answer is that Bethlehem[8] fulfilled the prophet Micah's seven-hundred-year-old promise:

> *But you, O Bethlehem Ephrathah, who are too little to be among the clans of Judah, from you shall come forth for Me one who is to be ruler in Israel, whose coming forth is from of old, from ancient days. Micah 5:2*

Missionary Dennis Hilgendorf, who served in the Middle East during most of his career and who, as a result, understood Mideastern culture well, believed that Joseph must have had relatives in Bethlehem. Because of the emphasis the Jews placed on family bloodlines, travelers were always welcome in the homes of relatives. But why, then, did Mary and Joseph look for a place to stay at an inn? Jewish law required that a woman found to be unfaithful be stoned or put to death (Leviticus 20:10; Deuteronomy

22:21). The same penalty applied to women who were not virgins on their wedding day. Because Joseph had not demanded Mary's execution or, at the very least, divorced her, Pastor Hilgendorf believed family members would have ostracized the couple.

As I toured the Holy Land some years ago, our group's guide showed us an inn near Bethlehem, typical of the first century. It was huge. In addition to the main "hotel," the complex included a high wall that encircled an area the size of a city block. Here travelers could keep their animals at night. Although Luke 2:7 says the inn (presumably the main building) was filled to capacity due to the census, couldn't Mary and Joseph have used at least a corner of the enclosed area? After all, they had traveled some seventy miles, and Mary was about to give birth!

We cannot know with any certainty, but perhaps the innkeeper refused this accommodation because he was concerned about the Old Testament laws that made anyone who came in contact with blood ceremonially unclean. Any chair or stool on which Mary sat and any bed on which she slept would have been made unclean by the blood that accompanies childbirth. No one else could have used it until it had been purified, resulting in a possible loss of business for the innkeeper.

The hills around Bethlehem contain numerous caves, often used by shepherds seeking shelter in inclement weather. I visited one on the tour. It was quite large and had a stone manger. It was also somewhat damp and a bit musty. If such a cave had sheltered cattle, sheep, or goats just prior to Mary and Joseph's arrival, or if animals were still being sheltered there, smelly animal droppings may have littered the floor. We don't know for sure, of course, that Mary and Joseph sought shelter in such a cave; Luke merely implies that the innkeeper directed the couple to a shelter and that it contained a manger that became our infant Savior's first bed.

Contrast that with the antiseptic birthing rooms in today's hospitals. Contrast it, too, with the manger scenes we create for Christmas pageants in our churches. We construct mangers from new wood and fill them with sweet-smelling hay. We focus spotlights on the scene and surround it with strings of tiny colored lights. Quite different from the reality Mary and Joseph experienced!

People often comment on the humiliation Jesus suffered as He hung dying on the cross like a common criminal. Actually, our Lord had humbled Himself from the first moment of His conception. His earthly lineage included Tamar, an unwed mother; Rahab, a prostitute or "madam"; Bathsheba, an adulteress; and Ruth, a non-Jewish foreigner. Although omnipresent and divine, God's Son willingly took on human flesh, willingly assumed the form of a servant. He descended from heaven's high throne to lie in a manger, to wear diapers changed by an unknown peasant girl. Yet, He remained King of the universe, with unimaginable grace as His true glory!

Mary: Chosen by God

How tired Mary must have felt as she and Joseph arrived in Bethlehem! How she must have wondered as she turned the angel Gabriel's words over and over in her mind and heart. The dream of every Jewish girl was undoubtedly that of becoming the mother of the promised Messiah—and Yahweh had chosen *her!*

Yes, Mary had been troubled and filled with wonder at the angel's first words, but Gabriel's explanation had been so reassuring: "Do not be afraid, Mary, for you have found favor with God." The child she would bear would be "great" and would be "called the Son of the Most High."

Mary believed the angel, but "How will this be, since I am a virgin?" she asked in bewilderment.

The angel's explanation satisfied her: "The Holy Spirit will come upon you, and the power of the Most High will overshadow you; therefore the child to be born will be called holy—the Son of God." Then the angel told her about Elizabeth, "who was called barren," yet now was in her sixth month of pregnancy.

Convinced that nothing is impossible with God, Mary's answer was one of complete trust and deep humility: "I am the servant of the Lord; let it be to me according to your word." With that, the angel left.

Now she was alone! Some teenagers would have found themselves shocked into complete silence. Some would have trembled or perhaps even fainted from fear. Some would have danced with joy and ecstasy, yearning to tell everyone—except, of course, who would have believed them?

The Blessing of Affirmation

How desolate and lonely Mary must have felt after the angel's visit! She had great news, news for which every believer, generation after generation, had been waiting! But whom could she tell? She was going to give birth to the Savior of the world! Would her family have believed her? Or would they have questioned her sanity? Would they have suspected her of being unfaithful to Joseph? With adultery as the only "reasonable" explanation for her condition, Mary's pregnancy would have disgraced her family and scandalized the neighborhood! To whom could she turn?

The angel had said Mary's relative Elizabeth was also miraculously pregnant. But Elizabeth and her husband, Zechariah, lived south of Jerusalem, a distance of nearly a hundred miles! Nevertheless, Mary got ready and hurried to their home, probably linking up with a passing caravan or a smaller group of travelers. It wasn't safe for a woman to travel alone!

Mary wasn't disappointed when she arrived:

> *When Elizabeth heard the greeting of Mary, the baby leaped in her womb. And Elizabeth was filled with the Holy Spirit, and she exclaimed with a loud cry, "Blessed are you among women, and blessed is the fruit of your womb!" Luke 1:41–42*

Affirmation at last! Even Elizabeth's baby leaped in recognition of the infant Mary would bear, and Elizabeth, who was "righteous before God," affirmed Mary for believing the angel's message. Yes, Elizabeth had no doubt about the identity of the tiny infant growing in Mary's womb. And Elizabeth's baby knew too! Elizabeth shouted with joy because "the mother of my Lord" had come to visit and because the long-awaited Savior of the world was now present, although *in utero*, in her home!

Mary responded by singing a song of praise to the Lord. Today we call it the Magnificat, and many Christian churches incorporate it into their worship services, often in Vespers. The longest set of words attributed to any woman in the New Testament, it reminds one of the song of Hannah (1 Samuel 2:1–10). Both psalms—for that is the genre into which they most readily fit—express joy in the Lord and trust in His mercy. Both describe the Lord's care for the poor and His compassion on the needy. Both recognize God's power in bringing down the haughty and elevating the humble. Correctly, Mary notes:

*From now on all generations will call me
blessed;*

*For He who is mighty has done great things
for me, and holy is His name.*

*And His mercy is for those who fear Him from
generation to generation. Luke 1:48b–50*

Nevertheless, life would not be easy for Mary. Imagine having to tell your betrothed you are pregnant—by the Holy Spirit! And *that* in a culture which carefully spelled out the penalties for adultery. Everyone in rural, agrarian Palestine knew virgin birth to be impossible! Yet, after Joseph learned of Mary's pregnancy, he decided not to expose her to public disgrace, let alone the much harsher penalties the law allowed. Instead, he would divorce her quietly. Even that would be socially punishing, a shame and disgrace in a society that cared about public opinion and one's reputation.

A betrothal in those days was a serious contract, negotiated by the parents of both the bride and the groom. Much more committed than what we know as engagement today, a betrothed couple was legally bound, yet the two did not live together. The fathers of both bride and groom held signed, legal documents committing the couple to each other for life and establishing the dowry—that is, the property the bride would bring into the marriage and the price the groom would pay to the bride's father to compensate for his loss. In fact, betrothals were tantamount to marriage, so much so that if a woman's betrothed died, society considered her a widow.[9]

On the wedding day, there was no formal ceremony like those today, although there might be a special blessing. When the groom had a home prepared for his bride—usually a room added on to his parents' house—he would come for her. Jesus' parable of the ten bridesmaids describes the custom (Matthew 25:1–13). Even if the bridegroom was delayed until midnight, a joyous procession would form, and the bride would be taken from her home to her new residence for the wedding feast.

Mary evidently told Joseph about her condition. And as he deliberated about what to do, an angel appeared to him in a dream, telling him not to be afraid to take Mary as his wife. The baby she was carrying truly had been conceived by the Holy Spirit. The child was to be called Jesus, a name Joseph would have recognized. It is the Greek version of the Hebrew name *Joshua*, which means "the Anointed One" or "Yahweh (the Lord, God of the covenant) is salvation."[10] This child would bear that name "because He will save His people from their sins" (Matthew 1:21). The child would also be called Immanuel, meaning "God with us" (v. 23), thus emphasizing His divine nature.

Joseph did as the angel directed, taking Mary home with him. Scripture gives no indication of a wedding dinner, and under the circumstances, there probably was none. Was Mary saddened by the lack of celebration, or was she simply happy to be home with Joseph and eagerly awaiting her very special baby?

Undoubtedly, thanks to Joseph's complete acceptance of the angel's advice, he was a great support to Mary. Both had received a remarkable message from the Lord, giving them a unique bond. Both knew God's promise of a Savior, and now at last the time was here. All of the Old Testament prophecies were coming true through the Spirit-conceived baby in Mary's womb.

Imagine becoming the earthly mother of the only Son of God! The challenge of raising any child can be overwhelming, but this baby, miraculously conceived, was both human and divine. He was the Son of God, sent to save the world. He was the long-awaited fulfillment of God's covenant promises to His people. How could a mere teenager with little experience in life hope to adequately mother the Son of God? How Mary must have prayed and clung to her faith as she replayed the angel's message over and over again in her mind. Scripture says she kept all these things in her heart and pondered them (Luke 2:19). And it's no wonder!

Nevertheless, as predicted (v. 35), Mary's life would prove difficult. Her unexpected pregnancy and her baby's birth in an animal shelter were only the beginning. Mary, Joseph, and the child Jesus would face the threat of death from insanely jealous King Herod (Matthew 2:1–12). Mary would suffer the anguish of losing her twelve-year-old son, and three days would pass before she received any word of His whereabouts or safety (Luke 2:41–51).

After He had grown to adulthood, she would hear about Him teaching things that angered hearers. At one point, her neighbors would even try to murder Him by throwing Him off a nearby cliff (Luke 4:28–30). Worst of all, she would watch as He died an excruciating death. No mother expects a child to die before she does, and certainly not in such a horrible manner!

But there would also be marvelous reassurances as well. The visit of the angels. The story of the shepherds. The adoration of the Magi. Jesus' amazing miracles. His resurrection. Strengthened by the same Holy Spirit who caused her miraculously to conceive, Mary remained steadfast as she kept thinking about all these things.[11]

The ups and downs of Mary's life came in quick succession after Jesus' birth. Shepherds watching their sheep in a nearby field heard the good news from an angel. They told of a large chorus of angelic beings who affirmed the first angel's message and then joined in praise of God:

> *"Glory to God in the highest, and on earth peace among those with whom He is pleased!"*
> *Luke 2:14*

Amazed and curious, the shepherds hurried to see the newborn baby. Then they, too, praised God!

The eighth day after Jesus' birth, Joseph circumcised the baby and gave Him the name Jesus as instructed by the angel. Then, after Mary's purification was completed as required by Leviticus 12, the couple took the child to Jerusalem to dedicate Him, their firstborn male, to the Lord and to offer the necessary sacrifices at the temple. Because they were poor, they brought two pigeons as their sacrifice. Custom required the priest to take their offering, wring the neck of one bird as a sin offering, and burn the other on the altar as whole burnt offering.[12]

Waiting in the temple that day were both Simeon and Anna. Having been told by God that he would see the Lord's Messiah before he died, Simeon recognized that Messiah in baby Jesus. He took the child in his arms and, rejoicing, blessed Him. Anna, whom Luke calls a "prophetess" (Luke 2:36), "began to give thanks to God and to speak of Him to all who were waiting for the redemption of Jerusalem" (v. 38).

Mary and Joseph marveled at what was said about their infant son (v. 33), but Simeon's words must have caused some consternation:

This child is appointed for the fall and rising of many in Israel, and for a sign that is opposed (and a sword will pierce through your own soul also), so that thoughts from many hearts may be revealed. Luke 2:34–35

A sword? "What does this mean?" Mary and Joseph must have wondered.

Returning to the house in Bethlehem where they were most likely living by this time, they eventually had more visitors—Wise Men, or Magi, from the East who came "to worship the King," as Matthew 2 tells us. Legend says these men were from Persia, modern-day Iran. Scripture does not say how many Magi came, but legend has set the number at three because of the three gifts they brought—gold, frankincense and myrrh. How shocked and unprepared would we feel if strangers from afar suddenly appeared at our door to worship our baby?

Unfortunately, though, the door of Mary and Joseph's house hadn't been their first stop. They had asked directions in Jerusalem, supposing to find the newborn King in the nation's capital city. King Herod was not amused, to say the least. When the Magi failed to return to his palace with information about the infant as he had instructed, Herod's jealousy and worry led him to infanticide. He ordered every boy age two and under in Bethlehem and the region surrounding it killed. Given Bethlehem's population today, we sometimes assume the slaughter of hundreds of infants. However, at the time, Bethlehem was a relatively small town, and the number of children killed may have been fewer than twenty. Even so, it represented a tragedy of great proportion for every victimized family and for the town itself.[13]

Before the massacre occurred, an angel warned Joseph in a dream to escape with his family to Egypt. He got up in the middle of the night to obey. Thus, while still in early childhood, Jesus became a refugee. He and His parents lived as immigrants in a foreign land, a country from which their ancestors had fled to escape slavery. This, too, happened in fulfillment of prophecy (Matthew 2:15).

After Herod died, Joseph learned in another dream that it was safe to return to Israel. However, since King Herod's son had succeeded him as ruler in Judea, Joseph chose to take his family back to Nazareth in Galilee, thus fulfilling another prophesy: "He shall be called a Nazarene" (v. 23).

Mary must have found it a relief to be back in her home country. There "the child grew and became strong, filled with wisdom. And the favor of God was upon Him" (Luke 2:40).

"Where Is He?"

As any mother knows, children often do surprising and unexpected things. Jesus was no exception.

Because Jewish men were required to attend the Feast of the Passover annually at the temple, Joseph made the trip each year. Jesus and Mary went along. Customarily, and for safety's sake, families traveled in caravans with relatives and neighbors. The parents all watched out for one another's children. If one optimistically assumes a group of families like this could cover about twenty miles a day, the journey from Nazareth to Jerusalem would have taken more than three days.

By the time Jesus was twelve years old, Mary and Joseph probably allowed Him a great deal of independence. He was nearing the point of adulthood as established by that culture. He was certainly becoming a responsible young man, and He surely would have known the time at which the caravan was to leave Jerusalem after the Feast concluded.

Consequently, Mary did not worry when, as the caravan got under way for the trip home, she did not see Jesus. She simply assumed He was with friends or with other relatives. But toward the end of the day, when He had not appeared, both parents began looking for Him. He was nowhere to be found. Imagine the panic!

Immediately, both Mary and Joseph returned to Jerusalem. For a full day, they could find no sign of Him. How worried Mary, especially, must have been! Finally they saw Him in the temple courts, "sitting among the teachers, listening to them and asking them questions" (Luke 2:46). His understanding amazed everyone and astounded His parents. As relief flooded over her, Mary immediately became practical. "Son, why have You treated us so? Behold, Your father and I have been searching for You in great distress," she scolded (v. 48).

In Jesus' response, we read the first words spoken by the Son of God in His earthly ministry: "Why were you looking for Me? Did you not know that I must be in My Father's house?" (v. 49). The Old Testament records only a handful of instances in which God is called by the personal title *Father* (compare Deuteronomy 32:6; Isaiah 63:16; Malachi 2:10), but *Father* is the precise term Jesus used! His choice of words reflects a deep consciousness of both His mission and His office. He "must" be there, obedient to Yahweh and beginning to invest His life for our salvation.

Luke indicates that Mary and Joseph did not understand what Jesus was saying, but again the holy writer tells us that Mary kept all these things in her heart. Perhaps she shuddered as she remembered Simeon's words about the "sword" that would "pierce her heart." Perhaps not. In any case, the sword would not strike that day.

Despite the apparent sharpness of Jesus' answer to Mary, He was not being disobedient or uncaring, for He was without sin (Hebrews 4:15). Rather, by age 12, He already realized the need to comply with His heavenly Father's will, and His explanation would have calmed Mary's worry and reminded her of His purpose and of His divinity. He returned to Nazareth with Mary and Joseph, and He "was submissive to them" (Luke 2:51). Luke describes our Lord's growth into adulthood in these words: "Jesus increased in wisdom and stature and in favor with God and man" (v. 52).

It's interesting to note that the detailed description Luke gives of this incident and especially of Jesus' response to Mary's question. Bible scholars believe that Mary herself was the source of Luke's information about Christ's childhood, information the Holy Spirit inspired Luke to record for us.

Seemingly Rebuked

For the next eighteen years, we hear no more about Mary or Jesus. Then, as from out of nowhere, Elizabeth's son, John the Baptizer, emerges from the desert near the Jordan River to begin preparing the people for Christ's appearance on the public scene.

Following His Baptism by John and forty days of temptation by Satan, Jesus Himself, now age 30, appeared and began to launch His public ministry. While attending a wedding celebration at Cana, Jesus performed His first miracle. Mary alerted Him to the fact that the wine supply was running low. (In some cases, wedding feasts lasted for several days.) At first it appeared that the Lord refused her request: "Woman, what does this have to do with Me? My hour has not yet come" (John 2:4).

Someone today who addressed his mother as "woman" would be considered disrespectful. But in that era, the title *woman* carried the same implied respect as *Ma'am* today. Even so, by these words, Jesus may have been signaling a change in their relationship, an indication that from that point forward, He intended to concentrate on fulfilling the purpose for which He had come to earth. Some scholars have pointed out that Jesus' use of the word *hour* in John's Gospel always points forward to His death. Taking that into account, the Lord may have been telling Mary something like "When I begin doing miracles, I begin the trek to the cross."[14]

In any case, the Lord's response seems not to have bothered Mary in the least. She tells the servants confidently, "Do whatever He tells you." Before long, Jesus pointed to six large stone water jars used for the ceremonial washings customarily performed both before and after meals. Jesus ordered them all filled with water. Each held between twenty and thirty gallons. When that was done, He asked the servants to take some of the liquid to the man in charge of the feast. He deemed it the best wine he had ever tasted! Where had it come from, he wanted to know. Customarily, the wedding couple would serve their best wine first, then follow it with cheaper wine after the guests had already drunk enough to dull their palates.

By this first miracle, Jesus "manifested His glory. And His disciples believed in Him" (v. 11). As He began His teaching tours, the number of His miracles continued to grow. Larger and larger crowds followed Him. Without doubt, word would have regularly reached Mary concerning her Son's message and ministry, His followers, and His detractors.

One day during Jesus' second tour of Galilee, His mother and brothers heard disturbing rumors. He was so focused, so engaged in His work, that He was not even taking time to eat! Concerned, they went to visit Him, planning to "seize Him" (Mark 3:21). "He's gone mad! He's out of His mind!" they had concluded.

When they arrived, such a large crowd blocked the door that they couldn't get inside the house where He was teaching. So they sent a messenger in to ask Him to come out to them. He responded, "Who are My mother and My brothers?" If His words sound confusing to us, they must have proven very difficult for Mary to understand. Mary had given birth to Him, loved Him, reared Him, cared for Him, taught Him, and suffered rejection because of Him. Was He now speaking as if she didn't exist, as if she weren't even related to Him?!

His answer, however, was not spoken as an insult to Mary. Rather, it blesses all believers by expanding the definition of family to include us. All who believe in Jesus belong to the family of God. We all are included in His family: "Whoever does the will of God, he is My brother and sister and mother" (v. 35.)

Jesus also emphasizes knowing and doing God's will in Luke 11:27–28. On that occasion, following the custom of the day in which people praised an individual by praising that person's mother, a woman commented to Jesus, "Blessed is the womb that bore You, and the breasts at which You nursed!" But Jesus answered, "Blessed rather are those who hear the word of God and keep it!"

Happiness often eludes parents. Mary, faithful to the end, must have felt as if her heart would break while she watched Jesus die the cruel death of Calvary. Although most of the male disciples had disappeared from the scene, John 19:25–27 tells us that Mary remained there with three other women—her sister, Mary the wife of Clopas, and Mary Magdalene.

Despite His suffering and agony during those last hours, Jesus never lost His sense of responsibility. By this time, Joseph was likely deceased. As the oldest son, Jesus was responsible for His mother's welfare. Hanging there, enduring the suffering for the sins of the entire world, it would have been so easy to ignore or forget His role in His earthly family. "Let My male relatives take care of her; I have bigger things to think about just now," He could have reasoned. Instead, Jesus demonstrated His love and compassion by asking one of His closest friends and disciples, John, to care for Mary as if she were his own mother. John did as the Lord asked, taking Mary into his home.

After Jesus' death, the disciples often gathered to pray as a group. This first congregation included Mary as well as other followers, including many women, according to Acts 1:14. Although Luke does not name those who gathered on the Day of Pentecost, he does tell us that all the believers were there. It's reasonable to assume that Mary must have been among those who received the gift of the Holy Spirit on that occasion. What a climax to the momentous days of her Son's death, burial, resurrection, and ascension. As He had promised, Jesus sent His Holy Spirit to them. From miracle birth to horrible death to miracles of resurrection and ascension, through it all, the Holy Spirit had kept Mary faithful, supportive, and trusting. Now she, like we ourselves, could enjoy His ongoing presence as the Spirit continued to provide hope and confidence through the Word and in the Sacrament.

Neither Scripture nor history tells us when and where Mary died. Members of the Orthodox Church teach that her death came a decade after the Lord's ascension. Several countries, including Israel, Turkey, and Pakistan, claim to have located her tomb within their borders. Some scholars believe John took Mary with him to Ephesus, the city he served as pastor and bishop for many years. If so, perhaps she was buried there. Tourists can visit a home near Ephesus where legend says she lived and a cemetery just outside the ruins of the city that purportedly holds her grave.

The Roles of a Mother

As we consider Mary's life, we realize how little we actually know about her. Her parents are not mentioned in Scripture; other sources identify them as Joachim and Anne. A church built next to the site of the Pool of Bethesda in Jerusalem is named the Church of St. Anne, perhaps in her mother's honor. Some believe that at the time of Mary's betrothal, Anne and Joachim may have lived in Sepphoris, an expanding community near Nazareth, and Joseph may have worked there—thus making it possible for Joseph and Mary to meet.

Sons usually learned the craft of their fathers, and that's apparently what Jesus did. Both He and Joseph are identified in Matthew 13:55 and Mark 6:3 by the Greek word *tekton*, meaning "a construction craftsman, skilled in wood and stone work." They were builders, not only carpenters.

Historians believe the town of Nazareth would have been too small to have kept two such craftsmen busy, so when necessary, Joseph and Jesus may have walked to Sepphoris for work. Although Sepphoris is not mentioned in Scripture, recent excavations have shown it to be the largest and most cosmopolitan city in all of Galilee. Herod Antipas used it as his administrative center for many years. It now is a national historical park.

Traditionally, Mary had no children after Jesus. Luther believed this. However, today, many scholars believe she had more children by Joseph. Matthew 13:55–56 mentions Jesus' "sisters" and gives the names of four "brothers": James, Joseph, Simon, and Judas. These may, however, have been cousins. The Greek words used can mean either siblings or cousins. Educating and rearing children, running the household, obtaining and preparing food, making clothes, doing the laundry by hand, and carrying water for daily household necessities left no spare time. (Nazareth has a spring, now identified as Mary's Fountain, which she may have used.)

Scripture extols the virtues of motherhood, and the commandment telling children to honor and obey their parents includes a promise: Those who do this will "live long in the land" (Ephesians 6:1–3). Further support for parents is found in Proverbs 1:8, "Hear, my son, your father's instruction, and forsake not your mother's teaching," and again in 6:20. Aging parents also find comfort in Proverbs 23:22: "Listen to your father who gave you life, and do not despise your mother when she is old."

Guidelines for Parenting

However, Scripture offers few specific rules for mothering and little explicit guidance for parenting. Two of the most frequently quoted verses are these:

> *Train up a child in the way he should go; even when he is old he will not depart from it.*
> *Proverbs 22:6*

> *Fathers, do not provoke your children to anger, but bring them up in the discipline and instruction of the Lord. Ephesians 6:4*

Deuteronomy 11:18–21 is more specific:

Lay up these words of Mine in your heart and in your soul, and you shall bind them as a sign on your hand, and they shall be as frontlets between your eyes. You shall teach them to your children, talking of them when you are sitting in your house, and when you are walking by the way, and when you lie down, and when you rise. You shall write them on the doorposts of your house and on your gates, that your days and the days of your children may be multiplied in the land that the LORD swore to your fathers to give them, as long as the heavens are above the earth.

Again, we see the importance God places on all people knowing His Word. (How did the ancient Jews tie God's words on their bodies? They placed them in small leather boxes, called "phylacteries," and with long, leather straps, tied one to the forehead and one to the arm during prayer times. Many Jewish people continue this custom today.)

Yet the Law of Moses made no provisions for schools. Homeschooling was the only option! Parents were expected to teach their children the Law of God at home. Over and over, families retold the history of God's involvement with His people until each individual knew it fully. Parents were to be diligent in this instruction, continuing it during all the ordinary activities of daily life, as seen in the passage above and in Deuteronomy 6:7. Fathers were required to teach the Torah (the first five books of the Old Testament) only to their sons. Nevertheless, while their education was voluntary and informal, girls, along with their fathers, mothers, and brothers, heard the Torah read and expounded publicly, and participated in both private and public prayer and worship.

When synagogues were established by the Jews during and after the Babylonian captivity, formal religion classes were held in them for boys, but any trade still had to be taught at home by the father. Beginning at age 5, boys learned to read and memorize the Torah, and at age 10, the study of the Oral Law began. Because there were no vowels in the Hebrew language at that time, "students had to listen intently to their teachers to catch the correct pronunciation of every word." The common languages of the day in Israel were Greek or Aramaic.[15]

Girls remained at home, learning homemaking from their mother. This included spinning, weaving, cooking, and treating illnesses—everything important to being a good wife and mother. In short, they learned how to manage the business affairs of the household, including buying food and fields, selling and trading, and serving the poor and needy, as seen in the exemplary woman of Proverbs 31. In addition to Scripture, they memorized Jewish history so they could teach it to their children, and the numerous ceremonial laws that would help them maintain a proper household, as well as prepare for feast days. They also learned to sing, and some became proficient at playing musical instruments.

During the second and third centuries, numerous apocryphal legends developed concerning Jesus' childhood. These continued into the Middle Ages. They described Jesus as mischievous and more—sliding down a sunbeam, playing tricks, and even causing the death of playmates who displeased Him. These are, of course, purely fanciful.

We know that throughout His earthly life, Jesus "learned obedience through what He suffered" (Hebrews 5:8). We also know that although He was tempted just as we are, our Lord never sinned (Hebrews 4:15). Instead, He lived the perfectly obedient life we could not live. He did this for us, vicariously, in our place. And now, God credits us with our Savior's perfect obedience.

Unlike Christ, we sin, and so do our children. My parents did not approve of spankings. My husband and I followed their pattern, administering a swat on the seat only when our children did something so dangerous that it posed a major threat, like running into the street when cars were coming. When they misbehaved, they had to sit on the couch for a given period of time. They still joke about how they quickly they wore out the couch.

It's so easy for parents to be overzealous, to want to raise perfect children. I'll never forget the day when I was once again correcting my son. He looked up pleadingly into my face and said, "Don't make me wrong again!"

How thankful we should be that God, our Father, understands us perfectly—He knows when we need discipline and when we need instruction by other methods. Paul's advice to Timothy illustrates the Lord's approach and offers an excellent guideline for us as parents: "Correct, rebuke and encourage—with great patience and careful instruction" (2 Timothy 4:2 NIV).

The God Who Comforts and Cares

Our heavenly Father understands and supports us in our role as mothers. He promises, "As one whom his mother comforts, so will I comfort you" (Isaiah 66:13). He wants to care for us "as a hen gathers her brood under her wings" (Luke 13:34). He asks reassuringly, "Can a woman forget her nursing child, that she should have no compassion on the son of her womb? Even these may forget, yet I will not forget you" (Isaiah 49:15).

And He warns us about keeping earthly family relationships in their proper perspective: "Whoever loves father or mother more than Me is not worthy of Me, and whoever loves son or daughter more than Me is not worthy of Me" (Matthew 10:37). Jesus must come first, and His Word must guide us, just as it gave Mary joy and enabled her to accept with trust and humility the miracle of the virgin birth and her role as the mother of her Lord (and ours).

Mary's song can be a reminder to us too: "He who is mighty has done great things for me, and holy is His name. And His mercy is for those who fear Him from generation to generation" (Luke 1:49–50). Mary recognized God's mercy toward her and accepted her awesome privilege with trust in the Lord's guidance. Today God offers each of us His mercy and grace also—through His Word and through the body and blood of His only Son, Mary's baby, who came to earth to pay the penalty of our sins and to assure all believers, women as well as men, of eternal life in heaven with Him.

The Heart of Jesus as Shown in Mary's Life

God loves each of us and wants us in heaven with Him. Through water and Word, believers become precious members of His family. To atone for our sins, His Son, Jesus Christ, willingly and humbly took on human flesh and endured temptation, persecution, torture, and death to give us—His chosen daughters—eternal life.

Chapter
THREE

Anna and Simon's Mother-in-Law

Senior Citizens, Grateful Servants

Luke 2:36–38; 4:38–39

And there was a prophetess, Anna. . . . She was advanced in years. . . . She did not depart from the temple, worshiping with fasting and prayer night and day. . . . She began to give thanks to God and to speak of Him to all who were waiting for the redemption of Jerusalem. Luke 2:36–38

[Jesus] left the synagogue and entered Simon's house. Now Simon's mother-in-law was ill with a high fever, and they appealed to Him on her behalf. And He stood over her and rebuked the fever, and it left her, and immediately she rose and began to serve them. Luke 4:38–39

Mothers-in-law provide lots of grist for comedians' monologues. A mother-in-law's over-involvement in family life can certainly cause trouble. This chapter focuses on one mother-in-law whose life and service reflect positively on the role—Simon Peter's mother-in-law.

The chapter focuses also on Anna, a single adult whose story would be unusual at any time in history. In our world today, especially, a woman who lived night and day in a cathedral would likely be arrested as a vagrant and jailed. Or she might wind up in a homeless shelter. Investigative reporters might even write human interest stories about her life. But as Anna served God in first-century Jerusalem, her life made a meaningful difference.

Luke introduces us to both these women, both elderly, and both honored to have interacted with God's promised Messiah—although in different cities and a generation apart.

Anna, a Prophetess

Scripture tells us that Anna "did not depart from the temple, worshiping with fasting and prayer night and day" (Luke 2:37). Her faithful vigil went on year by year until the day Joseph and Mary arrived to present the infant Jesus to the Lord and offer the required sacrifices. Scripture does not say whether Anna even had a home of her own.

Widowed at an early age, Anna would have again come under the authority of her father, Phanuel. By the time we meet Anna late in her life, Phanuel was most likely deceased. If Anna had no brothers or sons to care for her, she may indeed have been homeless.

Phanuel belonged to the tribe of Asher; his name means "happiness." Asher was the eighth son of Jacob. Anna may have been very beautiful; tradition reports that priests and princes often courted women from this tribe on account of their beauty.[16]

Scholars disagree about Anna's age. Some say she lived with her husband for seven years before becoming a widow and was, at the time she met Jesus, Mary, and Joseph, eighty-four years old. Others suggest she was married for seven years and then lived as a widow for eighty-four years. If this is accurate, and if she married at the typical age of 12 or 14, Anna may have been between 103 and 105 years old at this time. (Judith, the apocryphal book about a woman warrior who, like Deborah, saved her people from massacre, lived to age 105. Living that long may not have been so unusual.)

The Levitical holiness codes divided the temple complex into various "courts." Most likely, Anna would have been serving in the Court of the Women when the Holy Family arrived. Women were not allowed beyond that point. Simeon, a God-fearing man, was there too. Men were allowed in the Women's Court, and they could also pass through it into the next court, the Court of Israel, where they could watch the sacrifices burn on the altar. Only priests were permitted in the Court of Priests, which surrounded the temple proper. Gentiles worshiped in the Court of the Gentiles and were prohibited, on pain of death, from entering even the Women's Court.

Anna undoubtedly saw Simeon take the baby Jesus in his arms and praise the Lord for the infant, whom he described as "a light for revelation to the Gentiles, and for glory to Your people Israel" (Luke 2:32). As Simeon blessed Mary and Joseph and continued talking with them, Anna approached the group and gave thanks to God also. From that moment on, Luke tells us, she talked about the child to "all who were waiting for the redemption of Jerusalem" (v. 38). In doing this, she became the first woman to proclaim Christ publicly, to tell all who would listen that the promised Messiah had come.

What an amazing message Anna shared—a message of Good News for all who were looking forward to the fulfillment of God's promise to redeem Jerusalem. That included every Israelite!

That promise had been announced first by Yahweh Himself to Adam and Eve in Eden. There, God told the serpent, "I will put enmity between you and the woman, and between your offspring and her offspring; He shall bruise your head, and you shall bruise His heel" (Genesis 3:15). Anna no doubt knew that promise and the many other Old Testament writings that foretold the coming of Messiah.

Here are but a few:

- *God's promise to Abraham included this: "In you all the families of the earth shall be blessed." Genesis 12:3*

- *"The virgin shall conceive and bear a son, and shall call His name Immanuel." Isaiah 7:14*

- *"But you, O Bethlehem Ephrathah, who are too little to be among the clans of Judah, from you shall come forth for Me one who is to be ruler in Israel, whose coming forth is from of old, from ancient days." Micah 5:2*

- *"Shout aloud, O daughter of Jerusalem! Behold, your king is coming to you; righteous and having salvation is He, humble and mounted on a donkey." Zechariah 9:9*

- *"He was oppressed, and He was afflicted, yet He opened not His mouth; like a lamb that is led to the slaughter." Isaiah 53:7*

- *"He was wounded for our transgressions; He was crushed for our iniquities; upon Him was the chastisement that brought us peace, and with His stripes we are healed." Isaiah 53:5*

- *"Nor will You let Your Holy One see decay." Psalm 16:10b NIV*

- *"You ascended on high, leading a host of captives in Your train . . . that the LORD God may dwell there." Psalm 68:18*

These and many other verses, some written a thousand years before Christ came to earth, predicted and acclaimed His role among us. With the arrival of Jesus, those prophecies were fulfilled at last for Anna and for the world. The Savior was here! Her prayers had been answered! The Lord's promise to Simeon had been kept!

The joyous Anna could not help herself; she just had to give thanks and share this Good News!

Simon's Mother-in-Law

Luke also chronicles for us the service of another older woman (see also Mark 1:29–31; Matthew 8:14–15). Simon Peter's mother-in-law models for us the ideal of Christian service. In Christ's relationship with her, we also see His compassion for women.

As the story begins, she is ill and in bed with a high fever. It's bad enough to be sick when guests arrive, but in this case, the guest was Jesus, accompanied by James and John, Simon, and his brother Andrew. The four had just been called as Jesus' first disciples.

Arriving in Capernaum, where Simon's home was located, Jesus immediately went to the synagogue. There He taught and drove an evil spirit out of a man. As the time of worship ended, Simon invited everyone in Jesus' small retinue to his home. Some scholars believe it was close by—a hundred yards or so from the synagogue, in fact. Since the group did not learn of the mother-in-law's illness until they arrived, we know Simon did not invite Jesus with the intention of asking Him to heal her.

Without our understanding of fever as a symptom of an illness, people in New Testament days thought of "fever" as a disease in itself. Depending on its cause, the fever could have killed her without appropriate treatment.

Jesus went to her bed (probably simply a mat on the floor), took her hand, and helped her up. Immediately she was well—the first woman to be healed by the Savior. In gratitude for her improved health, the mother-in-law got up and helped the other women of the household serve their guests. We never learn her name. Nor do we know the name of Simon's wife, but Paul later tells us she was a believer and traveled with Simon at times (1 Corinthians 9:5).

The fact that Simon's mother-in-law lived in his home says a lot about Simon's concern for family. Most likely she was widowed or she would have lived in her own home with her husband. Upon his death, her sons or brothers would have been expected to take care of her. Maybe she had none, so Simon and his wife welcomed her. It was a generous and caring act—and a blessing for her in many ways. Not only did Jesus heal her on this occasion, but He likely visited the household as a frequent guest, and thus, everyone who lived there could have heard the Savior's teachings firsthand.

Naturally, the news about Jesus, His healing miracles, and His authoritative teaching that afternoon spread quickly throughout the entire region of Galilee. Mark tells us that by evening, as the sun was setting, "The whole city was gathered together at the door. And [Jesus] healed many who were sick with various diseases" (Mark 1:33). The whole town! Simon's mother-in-law not only had an "up-close" view of the evening's events, but she had the opportunity personally to vouch for Christ's miraculous power and kindness, His healing and compassion.

No Age Discrimination Here!

As these accounts of Anna and Simon's mother-in-law demonstrate, first-century culture did not discriminate against individuals on the basis of age. Not so in society today! Our society views aging as something to be avoided or delayed as long as possible. Magazines are full of advertisements for anti-aging products. Advertisers much prefer beauty queens over women with wrinkles. The culture in general admires athletic bodies over those slowed or stooped by age. The often-immoral behaviors of young movie stars draw more media attention than the profound thoughts of learned scientists, historians, and theologians.

In contrast, the Bible elevates white and gray hair as a sign of wisdom. In Anna we see the fulfillment of Proverbs 16:31: "Gray hair is a crown of glory; it is gained in a righteous life." Anna lived day and night at the temple, praying and fasting. Her dedication resulted in a firsthand opportunity to see, recognize, and bless the infant Savior—and then speak to others about Him.

Both Anna and Simon's mother-in-law knew God's command: "Serve the LORD with gladness!" (Psalm 100:2). Some have criticized Jesus for not urging Simon's mother-in-law to relax while the men served her. However, they overlook the fact that Jesus had made her perfectly well, had made her completely whole by His touch. She likely felt better at that moment than she had in many years. Her joy evoked a deep desire to do something for Jesus in return! How good it must have been to serve as a hostess for this special guest and His friends. How needed and important she must have felt!

Today, many seniors opt to work into years that used to be reserved for retirement. Some continue in the careers they have pursued over an entire lifetime. Others explore new fields. The Social Security Administration predicts that 30 percent of sixty-five- to seventy-year-olds will be gainfully employed by 2020. They will join 20 percent of people in their seventies. Some authorities estimate that nearly three-quarters of today's workers plan to work after they officially "retire." One-third of all retirees re-enter the job market within two years of retirement.

In part, this trend no doubt arises from financial need. However, part of it also reflects the fact that many seniors no longer feel needed after they officially retire. Senior residential communities often promote their facilities as worry-free environments. "We'll take care of you," they promise. Yet, unless residents have opportunities to continue using the skills they have acquired over a lifetime, unless they can apply their God-given abilities and the wisdom they have gained over the years, their bodies and brains soon atrophy. Society and the Church also lose.

Fortunately, the idea that retirees should have a responsibility-free life is changing as Baby Boomers reach retirement age. They are demanding that senior-living administrators consider the individual desires of residents, solicit their ideas, and help them maximize their God-given intellect and skills. As a result, there is increasing recognition that seniors still have a lot to offer as volunteers and mentors.

For example, Fairview Village, a Christian continuing-care retirement community in Downers Grove, Illinois, has established Project PEP (Program to Extend Productivity). Through PEP, the residents enjoy nearly two dozen interesting ways to stay involved in purposeful volunteer activities. Seniors living in this complex repair antiques and collectibles, engage in woodworking, practice creative arts, participate in the Fairview Chorus, serve as friendly visitors, research genealogies, work in both the gift shop and Granny's Resale Shop, reach out as helpful neighbors, deliver Meals on Wheels, serve as intergenerational tutors, volunteer in the library, teach English as a second language, and participate in the community in other helpful ways. The wide-ranging options demonstrate Fairview Village's belief that "longevity without purpose can be a curse."

Or consider Bethesda Lutheran Home in Watertown, Wisconsin. This institution also depends on its elderly friends to operate its numerous thrift stores, all of which play an important role in funding Bethesda's services to hundreds of developmentally disabled persons. One manager of Bethesda's Thrift Store in St. Paul, Minnesota, was ninety-two when she retired.

Women: Enabling Christian Growth, Reform

Service by senior women is nothing new. Throughout the history of Christianity, God has used the wisdom and work of dedicated women to advance His kingdom on earth. Here are a few examples:[17]

> **Helena** *(who died around AD 330), the mother of the Roman emperor Constantine, lived to be about eighty. In her last years, she traveled throughout the regions of Palestine and Sinai, encouraging the establishment and spread of the Christian faith. Sometimes called "the first female archeologist," Helena sought out the original locations associated with the life of Jesus and then oversaw the construction of the churches Constantine ordered built at Bethlehem, Calvary, Bethany, and the Mount of Olives to mark those sites.*

Paula *(347–404), a Roman matron, became a recognized Scripture translator. She studied Hebrew and assisted Jerome with his translation of the Bible from Hebrew and Greek into Latin. Known as the Vulgate, it remained the standard translation of the medieval Roman Catholic Church.*

Princess Olga of Kiev *(879–969) is credited with helping to prevent Russia from converting to Islam. When her grandson came to the throne, he adopted Christianity as the official religion of Russia.*

Margaret of Scotland *(1050?–1093) is known as the woman who "civilized" that country. Arriving there from England as a refugee, Margaret met and married King Malcolm III. Her godly influence transformed him, his court, and the nation. They took in orphans, invited the poor to dine at their table (as many as three hundred at a time), and set an example of personal worship for the court. They also founded churches, hospices, monasteries, and almshouses throughout the country. At her insistence, a council of church leaders was called to correct the religious abuses that abounded. To attract people to Christianity, she encouraged the start of new churches and improved existing ones.*

Hildegard of Bingen *(1098–1179), a powerful German abbess, was an outspoken evangelist, author, composer, musician, artist, doctor, theologian, and consultant to bishops, popes, and kings. Frustrated by the corruption of the Roman Catholic Church and the immorality of the clergy, Hildegard urged the people to repent and to depend on Scripture as their authority and on Christ for salvation.*

Catherine of Siena *(1347–1380) influenced popes, kings, and queens to support what she understood to be the will of God. One of her accomplishments was persuading the pope to return his headquarters from France to Rome, thus bringing a degree of peace to the warring Papal States in Italy. She did this fearlessly, she said, because she trusted in the Lord Jesus Christ, not in herself. She dared to tell one pope that he needed to control his temper, and she told another to be manly and stand up for what was right.*

Argula von Grumbach *(1492–1568), a writer and German "lobbyist" for the reformers, was a staunch supporter of Martin Luther. When an eighteen-year-old university student was arrested and forced to renounce his support for Luther's teachings, Argula challenged the school's actions. With the advent of the printing press, her letter regarding this situation was reproduced in pamphlet form, and her writings received widespread circulation. Luther referred to her as "Argula, the follower of Christ." For refusing to disavow the teachings of Luther, she was eventually banished from Bavaria.*

Katherine Zell *(1497–1562) served as a hospitable hostess to reformers. She married a Catholic priest who became a Lutheran pastor after he was excommunicated for marrying her. This led her to write a defense of clergy marriage. During one three-week period, sixty victims of religious persecution benefited from her hospitality at their parsonage. She also wrote hymns and campaigned for better-run hospitals.*

Elizabeth von Muenden *(1510–1558) In cooperation with male reformers in Germany, this evangelical (Lutheran) convert, writer, and reformer developed guidelines and orders of service for Protestant worship and wrote hymns.*

Corrie *(1892–1983) and* **Betsie Ten Boom** *(1885–1944), along with their brother Casper, were imprisoned for hiding and assisting Jewish refugees in their Netherlands home during World War II. Casper died after just ten days in prison, and Betsie died in Ravensbruck after several months. To the end of their lives, the siblings witnessed to their faith in Jesus Christ. After her release, Corrie traveled the world with the Gospel message.*

For Us Today

So what do the examples of these women, along with Anna and Simon's mother-in-law, have to say to women today?

For one thing, their life stories help us put our own lives into perspective. Each of us has been aging day by day since the moment of our conception! How much longer will we live here on earth? How much longer will we be able to serve our Lord? Only God knows.

Although some people lived to be nine hundred years old before the biblical flood, and a few reached the age of two hundred in subsequent centuries, historians tell us that average life expectancy declined to about twenty years by 1000 BC. Since then, it has been gradually increasing. In Psalm 90:9–10, Moses describes the normal human lifespan as about seventy years, while acknowledging that by God's blessing, some achieve the age of eighty.

By controlling the diseases of infancy and childhood, our nation has increased the average lifespan to nearly seventy-seven years. Some experts predict that over the next decades, we can expect larger numbers of people to live to age 110 or even 120! The number of centenarians and supercentenarians (people over age 110) continues to grow.

Nevertheless, life on earth is very brief. Scripture likens it to a fleeting shadow (1 Chronicles 29:15), to a swift weaver's shuttle (Job 7:6), and to grass that withers and flowers that fade in a single day (Psalm 90:5-6; 103:15–16; Isaiah 40:6–7). Yes, our time on earth is short, so we want to make the most of it. In response to God's love and the benefits He showers on us, we can

1. **Keep growing in the Word.** Growing old is a blessing when you continue to grow closer to God. What a joy to graduate from the milk to the meat of God's Word, from spiritual infancy to maturity (Hebrews 5:12–14). As we read, study, and hear God's Word, He draws us closer to Himself. His love, peace, and friendship give new meaning to our lives. This enables and encourages us to do an increasingly better job of telling others about Jesus, just as Anna did.

2. **Keep praying.** God invites all His people to "pray without ceasing" (1 Thessalonians 5:17). We may be tempted to think, why do I need to tell God about my problems every day? After all, He knows everything. I learned the answer to this question in a personal way one Mother's Day. I had not heard from my daughter, but because I had talked with her earlier in the week, I knew she was okay. However, she always sent a Mother's Day card, and none had come that year. Then my doorbell rang, and there she stood, flowers and card in hand. I enjoyed both the flowers and card; the

best present, though, was her presence. She stayed for a couple of hours, and we talked and talked, sharing joys, ideas, and dreams. Similarly, our Lord wants us to talk with Him! You might begin with the words of Psalm 90:12: "Teach us to number our days that we may get a heart of wisdom." With the same compassion Jesus showed Simon's mother-in-law, He attends to our every need, ever ready to listen and respond. We rest in His assurance, "Behold, I am with you always, to the end of the age" (Matthew 28:20).

3. **Keep serving.** As long as God keeps us here on earth, He has a purpose for us, just as He had for Anna and Simon's mother-in-law. The psalmist assures us, "The righteous flourish. . . . They still bear fruit in old age . . . [they] declare that the LORD is upright; He is my rock" (Psalm 92:12–15). As we serve, our Savior gives us the joy of bearing fruit in response to God's work in our lives and to the amazing love He showed by sending His only Son, Jesus Christ, to save us. With John, we affirm that "we love because He first loved us" (1 John 4:19). Seniors can speak of that love, pray for others, and serve as encouragers to everyone they encounter.

4. **Live a Christlike life.** As believers, we are the Body of Christ (1 Corinthians 12:27). Scripture tells us that the Holy Spirit gives each of us gifts to use for "the common good" (v. 7). What a privilege! Through the Holy Spirit, we are enabled to show compassion to the poor, weak, lonely, and needy in Christ's name. And we can tell them of His love. Jesus' infinite love and care extend to everyone, and He gives us the joy of "being His arms" as we serve them in His name.

5. **Remember our blessings and then tell others** how the Lord has helped us. Before printed Bibles were widely available, believers shared the story of God's faithfulness orally. The prophet Joel writes: "Tell your children

of it, and let your children tell their children, and their children to another generation" (Joel 1:3). What a privilege and a joy to share, to tell, to teach our children, our family members and acquaintances about Christ's love—and then to look forward to spending eternity with them in heaven.

As guardians of the faith history of their families, today's seniors can bless their descendants in another important way. Seniors can write a "spiritual life review" or record it on tape or disk.[18] Even if the young people of one's family profess no interest in Grandma's stories, they will have questions later, especially after the Lord has called the senior generation home. If there is no written or oral record, family members will have no way of knowing how the grandparents became Christians, what Christ meant in their lives, what peace their faith gave in the trials of life, and what assurance they enjoyed regarding eternity. This is an important, lasting way we can serve the Lord and share Christ with our family and friends.

Thus, we, too, can be Annas. Anna rejoiced because at last, God had come to her. She held the promised Savior in her very own arms! Jesus comes to us, too, in Word and Sacrament, bringing joy to our hearts and enabling us to tell others of His faithfulness.

Simon's mother-in-law provides another great example. Healed by Jesus, she rose to serve. Healed by the forgiveness of sins that flows from Christ's cross, we, too, respond with acts of love and service.

Jesus came to both of these women. His presence changed their lives forever. Because of that, they wanted to do something. Anna told others. Simon's mother-in-law served Jesus and His disciples. Jesus comes to us and changes our lives too. In His Word, in His Sacraments, He comes to us, heals us, and fulfills our need for a Savior.

How will you respond?

The Heart of Jesus as Shown in the Lives of Anna and Simon's Mother-in-Law

In Anna, we see the first woman outside the circle of Jesus' immediate family to recognize the Him as the Savior and publicly share the Good News. What a model for us! In His compassion for Simon's mother-in-law, we see our Lord's compassion for all women and His willingness to use His miraculous powers for their benefit. As Simon's mother-in-law eagerly served, so we find joy in our service as well!

The Widow and Her Son

Mourning Mother, Revitalized Woman
Luke 7:11–17

As [Jesus] drew near to the gate of the town, behold, a man who had died was being carried out, the only son of his mother, and she was a widow. . . . When the Lord saw her, He had compassion on her and said to her, "Do not weep." Then He came up and touched the bier, and the bearers stood still. And He said, "Young man, I say to you, arise." And the dead man sat up and began to speak, and Jesus gave him to his mother. Luke 7:12–15

One of the fascinating aspects of visiting the Holy Land is seeing the intermingling of the Old and New Testament sites. For example, Shunem was located on the southwestern side of Mount Moreh. There, Elisha restored the Shunammite woman's son to life. Less than two miles away, on the lower northwest slope of Mount Moreh, is

Nain, where Jesus raised a widow's son to life.

Of the thirty-five recorded miracles Jesus performed, three involved restoring life to someone who had died—Lazarus, the daughter of Jairus, and the son of the widow of Nain. In each case, Jesus acted purely out of compassion. As He saw the woman at Nain weeping, Luke tells us, "He had compassion on her" (Luke 7:13). Scripture mentions no words spoken, no pleas made as she saw Jesus coming, though she may not have known of Him or recognized Him. She offered no thanks after her son was restored, at least none Luke records. Perhaps the miracle so astonished her that it left her speechless. Most likely her gratitude showed in her demeanor and shone in her face.

Christ made no demands on her. Her son was alive, her desolation gone. In a real sense, she, too, had received her life back. Jesus had renewed her reasons for living, not to mention the restoration of the economic security she lost when her son died.

Certainly the miracle impressed the people who accompanied Jesus. Like readers of Luke's Gospel today, they must have noted the difference between the faith-filled plea of the Roman centurion, "Say the word, and let my servant be healed" (see vv. 1–10), and the unexpressed request of the widow. In both cases, Jesus proved His compassion and His divinity. Wanting to hear His every word and, possibly, to see more miracles, the large crowd followed the Lord as He walked from Capernaum to Nain.

It was not an easy trek! From Capernaum, Jesus would have followed the shore of the Sea of Galilee south through Gennesaret to Magdala, the home of Mary Magdalene. Moving westward from there, the road takes an 860-foot climb through a steep gorge. Imagine sheer cliffs towering on either side and caves dotting those cliffs and you'll readily picture the landscape Jesus and His followers would have seen as they made their way.

Tired and dusty after their twelve-mile journey, Jesus and His entourage approached the town gate of Nain. There they met a funeral procession. Because of the warm climate, the lack of embalming, and the fact that a corpse was considered ritually unclean, bodies were always buried within twenty-four hours of death. Among the Jews, even executed criminals were buried on the day they died, rather than, as in other cultures, being left to decompose publicly as an example to potential lawbreakers (Deuteronomy 21:22–23). Even so, no funerals took place on the Sabbath. That explains why Joseph of Arimathea and Nicodemus hurried to take Jesus' body down from the cross and place it inside the tomb on Good Friday before the Sabbath began with the setting sun.

Bodies of poor people were simply buried in the ground, possibly in a trench or a wooden coffin. Graves were marked by a pile of stones; there were no granite or marble headstones. To perpetuate the site, visitors or passersby would often add a stone to the stack. While I toured Israel, our group visited a cemetery on the Mount of Olives, just outside Jerusalem. Stones lay atop many of the cement slabs covering graves, the continuation of the custom that said, "Someone stopped by and cared."

Wealthy people in Jesus' day often purchased family tombs in caves outside of town or even sepulchers carved out of rock. These usually had space for from eight to thirteen bodies. Being buried among family members was important to Jewish people. As he lay dying, Jacob's last words included this request: "Bury me with my fathers in the cave . . . which Abraham bought . . . to possess as a burial place" (Genesis 49:29–30). Abraham and Sarah, Isaac and Rebekah, and Jacob's wife Leah already rested there. Verse 33 reports that after making this final wish clear, Jacob "breathed his last and was gathered to his people."

A year after the funeral, family members would often enter the burial cave, collect the bones, and place them in an ossuary—a small box engraved with the name of the deceased. The ossuary then remained in the cave. This custom made room for the next family member upon his or her death.

First-century Jews made every effort to treat the dead body with utmost respect. The body was never left alone; someone always attended it until its entombment or burial. The body was first washed and dried to remove any blood, dirt, or bodily fluids. Next, it was wrapped in pieces of linen cloth with spices between the layers. Because anyone who touched a corpse became ritually unclean, usually only one or two people undertook this task. (Acts 9:37 details these customs as they were practiced in regard to Dorcas.) We derive further insight from the fact that as Joseph and Nicodemus buried Jesus, they used seventy-five pounds of myrrh and aloe, and the women brought more spices on Sunday, intending to complete the process begun Friday evening. The spices masked the odors of decomposition.

Jewish culture did not allow for cremation; they considered it a heathen practice. Neither was there normally any mummification, as was practiced in Egypt, for that required removing some of the body's organs before the embalming process was begun. However, Joseph did have the physicians in his service embalm his father, Jacob (Genesis 50:2), and when Joseph died, he, too, was embalmed (v. 26).

Although some modern translations of the Nain story tell us the body lay in a coffin, the King James Version and the English Standard Version both use the word *bier*, a slab or stretcher designed for carrying a body. If burial was to have taken place in a cave or tomb, the body would have been carried on an open bier, then placed on a stone slab within the final resting place. If the body was to have been buried in the ground, a wooden coffin might have been used, the cover left off until the coffin lay in place at the gravesite. In either case, Jesus had no trouble reaching toward the body and touching it as He approached the procession.

Mourning and Mourners

As a funeral procession left a village, relatives, neighbors and friends—all the residents of a community—customarily joined the immediate family in a show of sympathy and from a sense of duty, whether or not they personally knew the deceased. A wealthy family would hire musicians and professional mourners, women who were expected to weep and wail. As Jeremiah wept over the exile imposed on the Northern Tribes by Assyria's army, he quoted the Lord as saying, "Call for the mourning women to come; send for the skillful women to come; let them make haste and raise a wailing over us, that our eyes may run down with tears and our eyelids flow with water" (Jeremiah 9:17–18).

Customarily, mourners also cut or tore a part of their clothing and continued to wear that garment throughout the mourning period. (Wearing old clothing was permissible.) Still today, Jews pin a black ribbon to their clothes, and some cut or tear that ribbon. Jewish writers describe the custom as a cathartic way to express the shock and rupture of death, "a visible tear which mirrors the inner tear that can never be repaired."[19]

As Jesus encountered the funeral procession at Nain, He had no trouble spotting the widowed mother. In addition to her obvious weeping, she would have been easily recognizable because she would have walked at the front of the procession. Traditionally in Galilee, female relatives walked in front of the funeral procession. Some scholars trace this custom to Eve's sin in Eden and to the death that sin brought into the creation.[20]

Ritual Impurity

Taking pity on the mother, Jesus approached the bier and placed His hand on it. This action, under Jewish law, made Him impure for a day. If He had touched the body too, it would have made Him unclean for a week. The purification process required by the Mosaic Law was quite specific:

> For the unclean they shall take some ashes of the burnt sin offering, and fresh water shall be added in a vessel. Then a clean person shall take hyssop and dip it in the water and sprinkle . . . whoever touched the bone, or the slain or the dead or the grave. And the clean person shall sprinkle it on the unclean on the third day and on the seventh day. Thus on the seventh day he shall cleanse him, and he shall wash his clothes and bathe himself in water, and at evening he shall be clean. If the man who is unclean does not cleanse himself, that person shall be cut off from the midst of the assembly, since he has defiled the sanctuary of the LORD. Numbers 19:17–20

"Get Up!"

However, at Nain, events took an unexpected turn. Rather than defiling Himself further by actually touching the body, Jesus restored life to the body death had defiled.

Jesus told the mother not to cry and then spoke life-giving words to her dead son: "Young man, I say to you, arise!" (Luke 7:14). Or, in a more direct translation: "Be risen!" To everyone's amazement, that's exactly what the dead man did, and "Jesus gave him back to his mother" (v. 15). Jesus did not simply help the young man up. In a tender, thoughtful gesture, He personally handed him to his mother. Her sad trip to the cemetery was no longer necessary; nor would she go home to the loneliness of an empty house.

The crowd was filled with fear—or "awe," as some translations put it. Everyone recognized that "a great prophet has appeared among us." They acknowledged, "God has come to help His people!" (v. 16 NIV). Not for centuries, not since the ministries of Elijah and Elisha, had someone been raised from the dead! The people were amazed. They had come to bury a young man and to support the grieving mother. Now her son was alive! Quickly the news spread throughout the surrounding countryside!

Importance of Children

For the widow, of course, the best part was having her son alive again. In that society, the importance of children, especially sons, was enormous. Sons supported their aging parents and saw to it that they received a proper burial. That's one of the reasons the psalmist says, "Children are a heritage from the LORD, the fruit of the womb a reward. Like arrows in the hand of a warrior are the children of one's youth. Blessed is the man who fills his quiver with them! He shall not be put to shame when he speaks with his enemies" (Psalm 127:3–5).

The firstborn son held a special place within Jewish families. Everyone saw him as the next head of the family. Greater responsibility fell on his shoulders from an early age. The oldest son customarily inherited a double portion of the estate when his father died. Nevertheless, because the Israelites believed that all life comes from God, they saw every baby as a blessing. While some nearby cultures abandoned handicapped babies and unwanted female infants outside the city walls, leaving them to die, the Israelites did not follow this pattern.

That's why Shiphrah and Puah, the Hebrew midwives, refused to follow the Egyptian pharaoh's order of infanticide at the time Moses was born (Exodus 1:15–21). The Jews' love of all children, including girls, is also evident in 2 Samuel 12:3, as Nathan rebuked David for causing the death of Uriah so he could take Bathsheba as his wife. Nathan told the story of a poor man who owned nothing but a little lamb. "It grew up with him and with his children. It used to . . . lie in his arms, and it was like a daughter to him," said the prophet.

If a family had no sons, daughters inherited the family's lands. This came about when the daughters of Zelophehad (Numbers 27:1–8) courageously took their case to Moses after their father died. They had no brothers, and they wanted their father's land to stay in their family. Moses took their request to the Lord, who decreed, "If a man dies and has no son, then you shall transfer his inheritance to his daughter. And if he has no daughter, then you shall give his inheritance to his brothers" (vv. 8–9). If there were no brothers, the land went to the nearest relative.

Options for Widows

"Nearest relative" did not include the wife. Thus, without her husband and without her son, the widow of Nain owned nothing and had no income. If her husband had a brother, the brother was expected to marry her and care for her. Any children born of that union were considered the first husband's heirs (Deuteronomy 25:5; Luke 20:28). Most likely, the widow of Nain had no brothers-in-law, and she may have been too old to conceive. That meant she would return to her father's household, as Orpah did after her husband, Naomi's son, died (Ruth 1:11–14). However, if the father of the widow of Nain was deceased and there were no other close relatives, she might easily become a homeless pauper.

After Naomi's husband and two sons died, Naomi returned to Bethlehem in Judah, where she still had relatives and property but apparently no one to provide her daily needs. She survived because her second daughter-in-law, Ruth, gleaned in the fields, gathering grain for her and Naomi to eat. Jewish laws related to farming made this provision for the poor:

> When you reap the harvest of your land, you shall not reap your field right up to its edge, neither shall you gather the gleanings after your harvest. And you shall not strip your vineyard bare, neither shall you gather the fallen grapes. . . . You shall leave them for the poor and for the sojourner. *Leviticus 19:9–10*

> When you reap the harvest in your field and forget a sheaf . . . you shall not go back to get it. It shall be for the sojourner, the fatherless, and the widow, that the LORD your God may bless you in all the work of your hands. When you beat your olive trees, you shall not go over them again. It shall be for the sojourner, the fatherless, and the widow. When you gather the grapes of your vineyard, you shall not strip it afterward. It shall be for the sojourner, the fatherless, and the widow. *Deuteronomy 24:19–21*

Without a daughter-in-law, the widow of Nain would have to do her own gleaning and then also depend on the goodness of other people and the tithes commanded in the law of Moses:

> *At the end of every three years you shall bring out all the tithe of your produce in the same year and lay it up within your towns. And the Levite, because he has no portion or inheritance with you, and the sojourner, the fatherless, and the widow, who are within your towns, shall come and eat and be filled, that the LORD your God may bless you in all the work of your hands that you do.* Deuteronomy 14:28–29

How desperate life could get for a widow reduced to this level of poverty is shown in the story of the widow of Zarephath (1 Kings 17:8–16). When Elijah asked her for bread, she replied, "I don't have any bread—only a handful of flour in a jar and a little oil in a jug. I am gathering a few sticks to take home and make a meal for myself and my son, that we may eat it—and die" (v. 12). At Elijah's request, she made a small cake of bread for him first; from that point on, although the famine continued, her supply of flour and oil did not run out. (Later her son became ill and died, and Elijah restored him to life.)

Elisha had a similar experience when he met a widow who had nothing in the cupboards to eat except a little oil. Her husband's creditor threatened to take her two boys as his slaves unless she paid his debt (2 Kings 4:1). At Elisha's direction, she borrowed many vessels and filled them all with oil from her meager supply, which miraculously kept flowing. When she sold the oil, she had more than enough to pay the debts. She used the remainder to support herself and her sons.

When Tabitha (Dorcas) died, all the widows in her community wept as they showed Peter the robes and other clothing Dorcas had made for them (Acts 9:39). Her death represented not just the loss of a friend, but also of a degree of economic well-being. Peter prayed, and the Lord brought Dorcas back to life.

Because of Jesus' compassion and power, however, the widow of Nain did not have to face the challenges experienced by these other widows. Instead, she had the joy of receiving her son back from death. And because of this inspired account recorded by Luke, we have the joy of knowing that we can look forward to "the resurrection of the body and the life everlasting," as the Apostles' Creed describes it.

The Challenge for Today's Christians

Although modern medicine saves many children from an early death, numerous parents, including widows, experience the sorrow of losing a child to death. No immediate, miraculous rescue brings these children back to life. Illness, accidents, and crime take far too many lives, far too often. Parents never expect a child to die before they do, and no woman expects to lose both a husband and a child. Yet, it happens—not just to nonbelievers, but also to people of faith.

When my first husband was just forty-six years old, he became ill one evening but went to work the next morning anyway because he felt responsible for an urgent project. Three hours later, two men from the company were at my door, informing me that he had died of a heart attack. Thirty years later, my oldest daughter, Linda, was working on a U.S. government project in Tanzania and had just been given a new assignment. In just three weeks, a labor center to help unemployed Tanzanians find jobs was being dedicated, and Linda was to make sure everything would be ready when the invited dignitaries arrived for the dedication. She began having headaches she attributed to stress, but the real cause was cerebral malaria. She died just four hours after being taken to the hospital by friends.

How do Christians survive such circumstances without losing their faith?

We surmount them because we have the blessing of knowing the rest of the story. Because of Jesus, we will see our believing relatives alive again—not temporarily here on earth, but eternally in heaven. Jesus demonstrated His power over death in the miracle at Nain, but He came to earth for an even greater purpose. Jesus came to die for us, to save us from our sins, to open the door to eternal life. Through His death, Christ conquered death once and for all.

It pleased God to punish Jesus instead of punishing us, His rebellious, disobedient servants. When Jesus shouted "It is finished," the will of God—our salvation, our sanctification, our adoption as His children—had become a reality. As John so eloquently says, "By this we know love, that He laid down His life for us" (1 John 3:16).[21]

By coming to earth as our Redeemer and Savior, Jesus showed us how much our triune God cares about us. God the Father was willing to sacrifice His own Son so that all who believe in Him will live with Him in perfect, resurrected bodies, forever in the new heaven and the new earth. Our God understands our sorrow; He knows what it's like to lose a child. As widows and as mothers of children who have died, we can talk with Him in prayer with the assurance that He hears and understands.

As the psalmist says (Psalm 68:5–6a NIV), "A father to the fatherless, a defender of widows, is God in His holy dwelling. God sets the lonely in families"—in His family! When we feel lonely and afraid, God says, "Fear not . . . the reproach of your widowhood you will remember no more. For your Maker is your husband—the LORD of hosts is His name" (Isaiah 54:4–5).

While that truth brings great comfort, we also need the touch of other human beings. That's where our families and friends come in. So often when someone dies, people shrink from meeting the bereaved. After my husband died, I was on the down escalator in a department store. Glancing into the aisle below, I saw a casual friend look up at me, then quickly turn and hurry down a different aisle. I'm sure she was afraid I might break into tears there in the store and cause an embarrassing scene.

At a Christian women's meeting a few weeks after my husband's death, I did feel the tears coming as the group began singing "Abide with Me!" When we got near the stanza I was dreading, "Hold Thou Thy cross before my closing eyes, Shine through the gloom, and point me to the skies," the woman sitting next to me noticed my discomfort (or so I assumed) and whispered a question on a different subject. How I appreciated her thoughtful gesture! Afterward, when I thanked her, she said, "But I didn't notice; I think my question must have been inspired by the Lord." Psalm 146:9 is accurate: The Lord does uphold the widow.

I did weep often at home and especially on one occasion when a friend gave me a ride to the airport. I was flying to a speaking engagement and was wondering if I would get through the talk without breaking down. My friend felt sad when her words triggered my tears, but it was a blessing to me because that incident got the tears out of my system, and the speech went well.

Friends and acquaintances should not hesitate to weep with a friend or to engage bereaved persons in conversation. A hug can help too. When a widow comes alone to church or to a social event, we can sit next to her. We can make regular phone calls and send notes. We can include her in activities. And we can pray for her and with her. God does indeed answer prayer!

Paul gives good advice to Timothy, advice designed by God to prepare him for his role as pastor:

> *Honor widows who are truly widows. But if a widow has children or grandchildren, let them first learn to show godliness to their own household and to make some return to their parents, for this is pleasing in the sight of God. . . . If any believing woman has relatives who are widows, let her care for them. Let the church not be burdened, so that it may care for those who are truly widows. 1 Timothy 5:3–4, 16*

Yes, families have a responsibility in all this—and so do the widows themselves! After my husband's death, I found the visits of a widowed neighbor so helpful. But I was embarrassed—I had not been there for her when her husband died. Reassuringly, she said, "Others were there for me, but when we endure a trial, God expects us to learn from it and then to be there for others who experience a similar need." Her words reflect 2 Corinthians 1:3–4. Here Scripture assures us that the "God of all comfort . . . comforts us in all our affliction, so that we may be able to comfort those who are in any affliction, with the comfort with which we ourselves are comforted by God." Comforted and consoled, we comfort and console others.

Heaven—Our Eternal Home

God's Word truly does sustain us! When life looks hopeless, we can turn to the One who gives us sure hope. Scripture not only teaches us about God's love, it promises us that God will wipe away all tears from our eyes. "Death shall be no more, neither shall there be mourning, nor crying, nor pain anymore, for the former things have passed away" (Revelation 21:4). What a glorious eternal home awaits all believers:

> *[It has] the glory of God, its radiance like a most*
> *rare jewel, like a jasper, clear as crystal. . . . The*
> *wall was built of jasper, while the city was pure*
> *gold, clear as glass. The foundations of the wall*
> *of the city were adorned with every kind of jew-*
> *el. . . . The twelve gates were twelve pearls, each*
> *of the gates made of a single pearl, and the street*
> *of the city was pure gold, transparent as glass.*
> *Revelation 21:11, 18–19, 21*

As widows and as bereaved mothers, we can remember the promises of God in Baptism and in the Scriptures. These assure us that those deceased loved ones who died in faith are already enjoying the presence of the Lord. As heirs of God the Father, as His beloved daughters, we can enthusiastically celebrate the gift of eternal life right now, here on earth (John 5:24; 1 John 5:11–13). And we can look forward to that "someday" when we have completed the tasks the Lord has given us to do, the day when we, too, will share the joy of life with Him and with our loved ones in heaven. All this is ours because our compassionate Christ has conquered death—the death of the widow's son, His own death, and our death—forever.

The Heart of Jesus As Seen in the Life of the Widow of Nain

When Jesus raised the young man from the dead, He demonstrated not just His power over death, but also His compassion for all suffering and grieving people. In the widow's experience, we are assured that Jesus cares for us, and we can confidently look to Christ as the true source of joy and peace, both for daily living and for the certain hope of life in heaven.

The Sinful Woman

Repentant Prostitute, Forgiven Believer
Luke 7:36–50

A woman of the city, who was a sinner, when she learned that [Jesus] was reclining at table in the Pharisee's house, brought an alabaster flask of ointment, and standing behind Him at His feet, weeping, she began to wet His feet with her tears and wiped them with the hair of her head and kissed his feet and anointed them with the ointment. . . . And He said to her, "Your sins are forgiven." Then those who were at table with Him began to say among themselves, "Who is this, who even forgives sins?" And He said to the woman, "Your faith has saved you; go in peace." Luke 7:37–38, 48–50

Teaching a class on justification and the forgiveness of sins to a group of developmentally disabled young men, a chaplain at Bethesda Lutheran Home in Watertown, Wisconsin, wanted to make sure they understood that big word *justification*. "When we are justified by Christ, it's 'just-as-if-I'd' never sinned," he said. Then he turned to a young man, whose usual response was to repeat the words of the instructor, and said, "In your *own* words now, tell me what it means to be forgiven and justified." Without speaking, the student got up, walked over to an open window, reached into his pocket, pulled out a handkerchief, waved it out the window, and joyfully shouted, "Bye-bye, sins!"

The sinful woman in Luke's story discovered this same joy in Jesus' forgiveness. It happened during a dinner at the home of Simon the Pharisee.

Who were the Pharisees? During the Second Temple period (between 516 BC and AD 70), at least four schools of thought emerged among Jewish leaders. Four groups represented these schools of thought—the Pharisees, Sadducees, Essenes, and Zealots.[22] As self-appointed keepers of the Mosaic Law, the Pharisees expected the Messiah to rule from Jerusalem as an earthly king, freeing the nation from Roman occupation. Believing that strict adherence to the Law of Moses was essential to salvation, the Pharisees added hundreds of customs and traditions to the Scripture itself. Known as the "oral law," these were designed to ensure that each person obeyed the written law to the letter. They emphasized not God's undeserved grace and the forgiveness of sin in the coming Messiah, but human effort. They taught and attempted to model strict adherence to the Law. As we study how the Gospels describe the words and behaviors of the Pharisees, we learn that most had fallen headlong into sins of self-righteousness and spiritual pride.

The Pharisee in Luke 18:11–12, for example, prayed: "God, I thank You that I am not like other men, extortioners, unjust, adulterers, or even like this tax collector. I fast twice a week; I give tithes of all that I get." Pharisees refused to associate with Gentiles, whom they saw as "too sinful." Nor would they speak with women in public, seemingly holding women in low esteem. Some historians have described them as the separatists or puritans of Judaism.

Although some Pharisees believed Jesus was who He said He was, the more He taught and the more popular He became, the more the Pharisees—or at least many of them—feared His influence. They saw Him undermining their authority and damaging their popularity with the people. Before long, they began to seek a way to eliminate Him as a competitor and critic.[23]

The Pharisees often invited prominent teachers to their homes for private dinners. We don't know whether Simon invited Jesus because he respected Him, because he honestly wanted to learn from Him, because he was curious about this new teacher's popularity, or because he wanted to catch Him in some act or comment that violated the Mosaic Law.

Dinner Etiquette Violated

Certainly Simon did not treat Jesus with the politeness that the hospitality of that day and time dictated. When Jesus arrived, no one washed His feet—a severe breach of etiquette. Neither did anyone provide water, making it possible for Jesus to do it Himself. Because the roads in Israel were unpaved and dusty and because everyone wore sandals or walked barefoot, their feet got dirty. As soon as they entered a home, sandals would be removed and the host (or, in wealthy households, a low-ranking servant) would wash each guest's feet. This also helped keep the house clean. The custom dated back at least as far as the time of Abraham. When three angels stopped at his tent (Genesis 18:4), Abraham water brought so they could wash their feet.

Adding a second insult, Simon failed to greet Jesus with the customary kiss, considered by that culture a respectful form of welcome. Five times the New Testament gives the directive to "Greet one another with a holy kiss."[24] Usually this meant a kiss on the cheek.

And third, no one anointed Jesus' head with oil. In the hot, dry climate of Palestine, Israelites rubbed olive oil on their skin, including their faces and heads (Deuteronomy 28:40; Psalm 104:15), and welcoming hosts would provide oil for this purpose as visitors arrived.

Party Crasher?

Before the dinner started, a woman "who lived a sinful life in that town" learned that Jesus would be eating there. Most likely she was a prostitute, a woman of the streets. How she got in, since this was a private party, is not known. Usually doorkeepers kept unwanted people out. However, wealthy individuals sometimes opened their homes to the poor. Some allowed anyone to attend and to listen to the conversation, but such visitors were expected to simply observe, remaining quiet.[25]

Simon's dinner was a formal event; the diners lay on couches around a low table rather than sitting on chairs or benches. Guests reclined, usually on their left elbows, sometimes supported by cushions, with their feet stretched out behind them. This custom made it easy for the sinful woman to kneel behind Jesus.

She was weeping, and her profuse tears wet His feet, washing the dust from them. Then she dried them with her hair and kissed them. She could use her hair in this way only if her head was uncovered, another indication that she was likely a prostitute. Proper women covered their heads.

She had brought with her an alabaster jar of perfume, most likely a tool of her trade. Proverbs 7:10 describes a wayward wife "dressed as a prostitute, wily of heart." Seductively she tells a young man, "I have spread my couch with coverings, colored linens from Egyptian linen; I have perfumed my bed with myrrh, aloes, and cinnamon" (vv. 16–17). Most alabaster was white; thus we speak today of "alabaster skin." When carved into thin pieces, it was translucent. Most likely this jar had been imported from the Far East or Egypt.

Although the culture did not condemn perfume as sinful, Simon's guests were appalled when this woman with a soiled reputation began pouring it on Jesus' feet! In fact, the whole idea of her touching Him was abhorrent to them. After all, rabbis avoided women in public. "[Simon] said to himself, 'If this man were a prophet, He would have known who and what sort of woman this is touching Him, for she is a sinner'" (Luke 7:39).

Jesus read Simon's thoughts. Immediately, He answered them with a story. Two men owed money to a lender. One owed five hundred denarii and the other, fifty. (A denarius represented about one day's wages.) Because neither had the funds to repay the loan, the lender cancelled both debts. "Now which of them will love him more?" Jesus asked. Simon gave the obvious answer: "The one . . . for whom he cancelled the larger debt" (vv. 42–43).

Then, pointing out Simon's omission of the ordinary acts of common courtesy, Jesus enumerated all that the woman had done for him. When He arrived, she greeted Him with a kiss. Then she washed His feet with her tears and kissed them repeatedly. She also anointed them with perfume. In an even more inflammatory exchange, Jesus announced, "Her sins, which are many, are forgiven—for she loved much. But he who is forgiven little, loves little."

Then Jesus absolved her: "Your sins are forgiven" (Luke 7:47–48).

Provoked, the other guests began talking among themselves, speculating about who Jesus really was—or thought He was. How could He forgive sins? Only God can do that! Jesus gave no explanation, but simply reassured the woman a second time: "Your faith has saved you; go in peace" (v. 50).

The Two Sides of Forgiveness

Forgiveness of sins! Priests could announce forgiveness after a penitent brought a sin offering to the temple and sacrificed the animal. But there had been no sacrifice here! Neither was there an overt confession of sins. How could Jesus absolve her? Simon's guests did not believe Jesus had authority on earth to forgive sins (Matthew 9:6). Christians believe it today because we know for sure who Jesus Christ is—the Son of our loving, heavenly Father, true God, the One who suffered and died to redeem us and who rose again and ascended into heaven. We know that He now sends His Holy Spirit to help us in our personal struggle with sin and with forgiving those who sin against us.

In the Lord's Prayer, we see the two sides of forgiveness—God's forgiveness of our sins and our response in forgiving the sins of others: "Forgive us our sins as we forgive those who sin against us." *As we forgive those who sin against us—that's* the challenge. Apart from Christ, true forgiveness is impossible. Only because God has forgiven us through Christ's sacrifice on the cross are we able willingly and joyfully to forgive others. "We love because He first loved us" (1 John 4:19).

It's much easier to judge than to forgive:

- "She did this!"
- "He said that!"
- "It's all her fault!"
- "They hurt my feelings!"

We all want respect, and that desire has recently added a new word, *diss* (short for *disrespect*), to our vocabulary. In some cultures, when one person "disses" another, a fight or even a murder may result. Make a mistake as you drive, and you may find another driver sideswiping you, banging your bumper, or shooting at your vehicle in a fit of road rage. An eye for an eye!

We all sin. We all hurt others in our words and by our actions. We all offend a holy God, failing to trust and worship Him as we should. But in Christ, we are forgiven. And in Christ, we *can* forgive. How often should we forgive? Peter once asked Jesus, "'Lord, how often will my brother sin against me, and I forgive him? As many as seven times?' Jesus said to him, 'I do not say to you seven times, but seventy times seven'" (Matthew 18:21–22). Yet, for the sake of His Son, God forgives us that many times—and more! He promises, "If we confess our sins, He is faithful and just to forgive us our sins and to cleanse us from all unrighteousness" (1 John 1:9).

Listen to how Scripture connects the two sides of forgiveness:

- *If you forgive others their trespasses, your heavenly Father will also forgive you, but if you do not forgive others their trespasses, neither will your Father forgive your trespasses. Matthew 6:14–15*
- *Whenever you stand praying, forgive, if you have*

anything against anyone, so that your Father also who is in heaven may forgive you your trespasses. Mark 11:25

- *Judge not, and you will not be judged; condemn not, and you will not be condemned; forgive, and you will be forgiven. Luke 6:37*

- *[Bear] with one another and, if one has a complaint against another, [forgive] each other; as the Lord has forgiven you, so you also must forgive. Colossians 3:13*

That's not to say that when we forgive others, God is required to forgive us, as if His forgiving our sins were some kind of a reward. Rather, by virtue of God's forgiving us for Jesus' sake, we are enabled and inspired to forgive. When we willfully and stubbornly withhold our forgiveness from others, we say to God that we no longer desire His forgiveness. True, forgiving others may difficult, especially when they have hurt us deeply, but the Holy Spirit helps us in our weaknesses, enabling us to say with gentleness and authenticity, "I forgive you." Scripture provides us many examples, illustrating that down through history, God has indeed helped His people forgive those who have sinned against them:

- *Esau forgave Jacob even though Jacob had stolen his birthright (Genesis 33:1–4).*

- *Joseph forgave his brothers for selling him, and when they came to Egypt to buy grain, he informed them, "God sent me before you to preserve life" (Genesis 45:5).*

- *David forgave Saul for trying to kill him (1 Samuel 24:8–12).*

- *Stephen forgave those who stoned him to death: "Falling to his knees he cried out with a loud voice, 'Lord, do not hold this sin against them'"* (Acts 7:60).

- *Even when everyone deserted Paul, he still prayed for them: "May it not be charged against them!" (2 Timothy 4:16).*

While Jesus hung dying on the cross, He demonstrated the power and extent of God's forgiveness, forgiveness available to everyone, everywhere, and at any time: "Father, forgive them, for they know not what they do" (Luke 23:34). As believers, forgiveness is available for us every day, every moment of our lives, because our Savior went to the cross for us. Out of His amazing love and compassion for us, our Lord sent His Son, His beloved and only Son, to suffer and die for our sins. Now, He freely offers that forgiveness to us in the Gospel, in the Absolution, in Baptism, and in the Lord's Supper. Through these means of grace, God forgives, renews, and sustains us. His love toward us then bubbles over into the lives of others.

Our Challenge: Personal Repentance

Acknowledging and repenting of our own sins, how-ever, can be just as difficult as forgiving others. It is much easier to dwell on the failures of others than on our own. Pride creeps in. Few of us like to admit we are wrong. Confession may mean immediate and embarrassing punish-ment. Nevertheless, Scripture urges us to examine our lives, confess our faults, and then, forgiven by Christ and empow-ered by Him, sincerely seek to do better.

Simon and his guests focused so tightly on the sins of the woman that they overlooked their own. Jesus had to point out Simon's shortcomings to him, but even then, we see no record of any apology.

Until at least the 1950s, formal confession of sins played an important role in many churches. Before taking Holy Communion, we Lutherans went to the pastor's office or home to "register." There we were supposed talk over our sins and shortcomings. That's not easy for most of us. While in college, some of my Roman Catholic friends would sometimes tell me before going to confession, "I have to think of something to confess." Today, many believers have a renewed appreciation for the value of private confession and absolution.

No doubt the sinful woman in Luke 7 was deeply aware of her sins and deeply sorry for them. The whole town knew! Her tears were her confession. They flowed so heavily that they washed Jesus' feet. How often do we weep over our sins? Would we have the courage this woman showed, risking public humiliation and possibly even abuse, as she moved forward to minister in gratitude to Jesus in front of the group of powerful men gathered there that day?

What relief, what freedom she must have felt when she heard Christ Himself say, "Your sins are forgiven. . . . Your faith has saved you; go in peace."

Peace—the kind of peace that only forgiveness can bring—is something we all desire but that some people never really and totally enjoy. Some of us confess the same sinful act again and again, refusing to believe that God actually forgave us the first time we confessed.

Unfortunately, some of us never forget our sins, even after God has forgiven them, even after we have repeatedly said "bye-bye" to them. We allow the wind to blow them back, and we pick them up and begin carrying the heavy burden again. We are like the lady in the elevator who refused to set down her shopping bags and allow the elevator to lift them to the next floor.

Others of us are humbled into inaction by our sins.

Instead of recognizing, confessing, repenting, and forgetting our sins, we become so consumed by our unworthiness, so overwhelmed by our sinful condition, that we fail to live out God's purpose for our lives, fail to use the gifts and talents He has given us in productive ways. If we see ourselves exclusively as poor, wretched sinners, we easily assume that we cannot chair a committee, act as its secretary, call on newcomers, or serve in any special capacity in our congregation. Consequently, we miss the peace and joy that our Lord's unconditional forgiveness and His subsequent invitation to service offer.

Galatians 5:1 puts it so beautifully: "For freedom Christ has set us free; stand firm therefore, and do not submit again to a yoke of slavery." In other words, don't be held hostage by the Law, by your sin, or by your failure to forgive yourself.

Welcoming Sinners

One week, members of a very proper church were startled to see two very unkempt, homeless-looking people enter the sanctuary just before the Sunday service began. No one moved to make room for them as they walked down the aisle, so the pair simply sat down on the floor in front of the first pew. A few minutes later, a gray-haired elder hobbled down the aisle, leaning on his cane. Murmurs of approval went through the congregation. "He'll let them know we don't sit on the floor here and don't welcome people dressed like that!" they assumed. The murmurs turned to shock as the aged gentleman reached the front and slowly lowered his creaky body to the floor to join the newcomers.

When we strongly adhere to rules and customs, to our routines and habits, we often fail to reach out with Christ's compassion to other sinners and to people who are different from us. Do we reach out in friendship to people who "aren't like us"? to people who come to us for guidance, information, or friendship? Do we know where to find help for them when they seek it? Is our church committed to reaching out? Have we encouraged and enabled our pastor and our leaders to take courses to learn how to meet the needs of all kinds of people in our community?

Or do we, like Simon, react with smug aloofness to the strangers and overt sinners in our midst while ignoring our own sins, the less public sins of "good Christians"? James 2:10 tells us that if we break one commandment, we have broken them all. Just as a piece of porcelain with a crack or chip is no longer perfect, so we too—all of us—fail the perfection test. How thankful we can be that the Perfect One took our place on the cross, that He welcomed and pardoned the woman described in Luke 7, and that He welcomes us with the same pardon, freely given and wthout measure!

Prostitution—A Perennial Sin

We don't know exactly what Simon's sins were, nor do we know for sure that the woman was a prostitute. Whatever the case, circumstances do not excuse sin, but understanding them may help believers to forgive sinners and encourage them to repentance, forgiveness, redemption, and rehabilitation.

If the sinful woman was a prostitute, we might wonder why she had not been stoned. Historians believe that the Jews did not always follow the command in the Mosaic Law that mandated that penalty. For one thing, Roman law did not permit the Jewish authorities to carry out capital punishment—that's why Jesus had to be handed over to Pilate for execution. For another, there may have been too many prostitutes in Israel at the time, and they may have done too much business, perhaps even with the religious authorities.

However, when the Pharisees wanted to trap Jesus in a violation of the Law, they brought to Him a woman who had been caught in adultery. Reminding Him that "Moses commanded us to stone such women," they asked, "So what do you say?" The Lord solved the problem by suggesting, "Let him who is without sin among you be the first to throw a stone at her." No one did, and one by one, they all sneaked away (John 8:4–9).

Later, when the chief priests and elders questioned Jesus' authority in spiritual matters, He spoke about the importance of doing God's will and again emphasized the blessing the Father would pour out on repentant prostitutes who placed their hope in the Messiah:

> *Truly, I say to you, the tax collectors and the prostitutes go into the kingdom of God before you. For John came to you in the way of righteousness, and you did not believe him, but the tax collectors and the prostitutes believed him. And even when you saw it, you did not afterward change your minds and believe him. Matthew 21:31b–32*

If the woman of Luke 7 was a prostitute, she was not the first practitioner of "the world's oldest profession" used by God to illustrate His generous, forgiving heart. The Book of Hosea chronicles the story of the prophet Hosea who married Gomer. Subsequently, Gomer prostituted herself, abandoning the home and marriage Hosea had provided for her. God used this as an example of His wayward people: "The land commits great whoredom by forsaking the LORD," He explained (Hosea 1:2).

Whatever her sins, the woman in Luke 7 had come to

realize their seriousness and was sincerely sorry for them. She also knew that Jesus was relieving people of their burdens of guilt and illness. Might He turn her life around too? She determined to find out, and when she heard He had come to her town and to Simon's house, she decided to go hear Him.

She was not disappointed. "Your sins are forgiven"— what glorious words! At first blush, Jesus' explanation of this forgiveness seems to attribute it to the love she showed to Him. However, this contradicts the rest of Scripture. For example, Paul writes to Titus, "When the goodness and loving kindness of God our Savior appeared, He saved us, not because of works done by us in righteousness, but according to His own mercy" (Titus 3:4–5; see also Ephesians 2:8–9).

The answer to this seeming contradiction can be found in James 2:26: "Faith apart from works is dead." God had given this woman living faith! That faith evidenced itself in her care and concern for Jesus. He recognized that her tears were real, that her heart overflowed with thankfulness for God's gift of mercy. Jesus knew what was in her heart— just as He also knows our hearts. We cannot fool Him by pretending to be something we are not.

Unfortunately, in every age, people have attended church on Sunday and lived no differently than the unbelievers around them the rest of the week. It's still true today, and because of it, many young people say, "I believe in Jesus Christ, but don't call me Christian!" To them, the word *Christianity* has developed negative connotations.[26] They caricature Christians as hypocritical, judgmental, too political, too focused on gaining converts, too sheltered from the real challenges and hurts of the real world. They often fail to see Christ dwelling in us.

Perfectionistic? Naïve? A bit self-righteous? Yes, they

are this and more. But that does not excuse us from the need for self-examination and lives of ongoing repentance and faith. In fact, it provides added motivation to demonstrate Christ's compassion and forgiveness in our every relationship. We humbly reach out to serve others, even as the sinful woman reached out in love to serve Jesus. Paul explains it this way: "The fruit of the Spirit is love, joy, peace, patience, kindness, goodness, faithfulness, gentleness, self-control; against such things there is no law. . . . If we live by the Spirit, let us also walk by the Spirit" (Galatians 5:22–23, 25).

Foot Washing—Loving Service

The nameless woman in Luke 7 served by washing Jesus' feet. The Bible includes numerous other instances of foot washing, and the practice deserves closer examination. Besides Abraham's offering water for foot washing to the angels (Genesis 18:4), we learn from Scripture that

- *Lot invited the two angels who visited Sodom to wash their feet and spend the night at his house (Genesis 19:2).*

- *Abraham's servant, sent by Abraham to find a wife for Isaac, was welcomed by Laban, who provided water for him and his men to wash their feet (Genesis 24:32).*

- *Joseph's servant offered water for foot washing to Joseph's brothers who had come to Egypt to buy grain (Genesis 43:24).*

- *"The LORD said to Moses, 'You shall make a basin of bronze, with its stand of bronze, for washing. You shall put it between the tent of meeting and the altar, and you shall put water in it, with which Aaron and his sons shall wash their hands and their feet. When they go into the tent of meeting, or when they come near the altar to minister, to burn a food offering to the LORD, they shall wash with water, so that they may not die. They shall wash their hands and feet, so that they may not die. It shall be a statute forever to them, even to him and to his offspring throughout their generations"' (Exodus 30:17–21).*

- *God's people followed these directions. Exodus 38:8 indicates that "He made the basin of bronze and its stand of bronze, from the mirrors of the ministering women who ministered in the entrance of the tent of meeting." Later, when Solomon built the temple, it included a "sea" of cast metal that held three thousand baths (about 17,500 gallons) and was used by the priests for washing (2 Chronicles 4:2–5, 7).*

- *An old man in Gibeah hosted three travelers (a Levite, his servant, and his concubine) in his home, and "they washed their feet, and ate and drank" (Judges 19:16–21).*

- *Abigail welcomed David's servant who had come with his master's proposal of marriage. In acceptance, Abigail said, "Behold, your handmaid is a servant to wash the feet of the servants of my lord" (1 Samuel 25:41).*

- *After washing His disciples' feet, Jesus told them, "If I then, your Lord and Teacher, have washed your feet, you also ought to wash one another's feet" (John 13:14).*

In the Western Church today, with few exceptions, Christians no longer practice the custom of foot washing. This is not simply due to the fact that most of us wear shoes and walk on concrete. The more important reason is that Christ's death changed everything. Pointing to the various Old Testament ceremonial washings, Hebrews 9:10

describes them as "regulations for the body imposed until the time of reformation."

When Christians do practice the custom today, foot washing memorializes Christ's servanthood and exemplifies humility. Some denominations incorporate foot-washing ceremonies into their Maundy Thursday services, recalling the occasion on which Jesus washed the disciples' feet. Each year on Holy Thursday, the pope washes the feet of twelve men to commemorate Christ's gesture of humility on the night before He died. At Lutheran gatherings, deaconesses sometimes offer foot washing to demonstrate their desire to assist and lead the Church in caring for the poor, marginalized, powerless people whom it would be so easy to forget. Quoting John 13:14, the Lutheran Deaconess Association explains, "When Jesus took the towel and basin and stooped to wash the disciples' feet, He provided a most vivid picture of servanthood and a model for deaconess ministry."

As the sinful woman washed Jesus' feet, she modeled the sincere repentance and humility that never goes out of date for God's people. Such repentance and humility remain essential for us in every generation. The blessing of forgiveness, given to us freely in the cross and empty tomb of our Savior, brings with it the gift of true repentance. Our Savior's forgiveness changes our lives forever! Forgiven, we can rejoice in the Lord always (Philippians 4:4). Forgiven, we can love the Lord our God with all our heart and soul and strength and mind (Luke 10:27). Forgiven, we can serve the Lord with gladness (Psalm 100:2). Forgiven, we can willingly forgive others (Ephesians 4:32). Forgiven, we can enthusiastically go and tell the good news of Christ's victory over death (Matthew 28:10). Forgiven, we can rest in Christ's peace (Luke 7:50).

The Heart of Jesus as Shown in the Sinful Woman's Life

God forgives us fully and freely through the work of His Son, Jesus Christ. That pardon moves us to joy and service. Thankful, we offer our Lord's forgiveness to others in His name.

Chapter SIX

Mary Magdalene, Joanna, and Susanna

Faithful Servants, Willing Supporters
Luke 8:1–3

Soon afterward [Jesus] went on through cities and villages, proclaiming and bringing the good news of the kingdom of God. And the twelve were with Him, and also some women who had been healed of evil spirits and infirmities: Mary, called Magdalene, from whom seven demons had gone out, and Joanna, the wife of Chuza, Herod's household manager, and Susanna, and many others, who provided for them out of their means. Luke 8:1–3

Servant. The word implies lowliness and humility. It's an uncomfortable concept for most of us. Rather than serve, we like to be served. Yet serve is what Mary Magdalene,

Joanna, and Susanna did voluntarily and gratefully. That's also what women throughout history have been because of what Christ did for them. In gratitude for Christ's compassion, acceptance, forgiveness, healing, and equal treatment, innumerable women have laid down their lives as martyrs, missionaries, and servants to the needy.

Though we know little about the three women mentioned in Luke 8:1–3, we do know that by allowing them and other women to accompany Him on His journeys, Jesus likely shocked many people. We've become accustomed to the fact that our Lord welcomed all kinds of people from every walk—tax collectors, prostitutes, lepers, Gentiles. But in His lifetime, this open-hearted attitude broke with cultural tradition in an unprecedented way, especially for women.

Throughout Israel's history, Jewish women and children were expected to attend the public reading of the Mosaic Law (Deuteronomy 31:12; Joshua 8:35). Women publicly praised the Lord with songs, tambourines, and dancing. Examples include Miriam (Exodus 15:20); Jephthah's daughter, who greeted her father as he returned home after his victory over the Ammonites (Judges 11:34); the women who greeted King Saul "singing and dancing, . . . with tambourines, with songs of joy, and with musical instruments" after David killed Goliath (1 Samuel 18:6), and the 245 men and women who sang in choir after the wall of Jerusalem was rebuilt (Nehemiah 7:67).

Like men, women could also take a Nazirite vow to demonstrate their desire to draw close to God and to separate themselves from the comforts and pleasures of this world. The vow required that they abstain from fermented drinks and from any food connected with grapes, avoid dead bodies, and allow their hair to grow without cutting it.

Some women were even chosen by God for special roles. Old Testament prophetesses included Miriam (Exodus 15:20), Deborah (Judges 4:4), Huldah (2 Kings 22:14–22; 2 Chronicles 34:22–28), and Isaiah's wife (Isaiah 8:3). (Noadiah, in Nehemiah 6:14, was a false prophetess.) Among "the wise," another category of leaders respected by the Hebrews (see Jeremiah 18:18), were the Wise Women of Tekoa (2 Samuel 14:1–3) and the Wise Woman of Abel (2 Samuel 20:15–17). Women also served at the entrance to the Tent of Meeting, according to Exodus 38:8. What they did there is unknown, but these women are mentioned again in 1 Samuel 2:22, where we learn that the wicked sons of Eli the priest were having sex with them. This displeased God so much that He arranged for both sons to die on the same day.

Examples of Unequal Treatment

Other than the exceptions noted above, women had little public visibility in the Jewish culture.

- *Their domain was the home. However, girls received no education outside the home as boys did.*

- *In matters of worship, as the* Jewish Encyclopedia *says, "The Temple proper might be entered by men only."[27] Although women had their own court in which to worship, it was also open to men, and the contribution vessels used by everyone were located there.*

- *Fathers could sell their children as servants. Eventually, the sons could go free, but not the daughters (Exodus 21:7).*

- *Men could have other wives and concubines, but a bride who was not a virgin could be stoned (Deuteronomy 22:20).*

- *Although men could divorce their wives for a variety of reasons, a woman could leave her husband only if he married another woman and then deprived her of food, clothing, and marital rights (Exodus 21:11).*

Nevertheless, the Law of Moses did provide protections to women unknown in most of the world at that time (and in many places still today). Even that Exodus passage cited above offers protections to the daughter:

> *When a man sells his daughter as a slave, she shall not go out as the male slaves do. If she does not please her master, who has designated her for himself, then he shall let her be redeemed. He shall have no right to sell her to a foreign people, since he has broken faith with her. If he designates her for his son, he shall deal with her as with a daughter. If he takes another wife to himself, he shall not diminish her food, her clothing, or her marital rights. And if he does not do these three things for her, she shall go out for nothing, without payment of money.*

On the surface, this would seem to be a horrific provision. How could a holy, just, loving God allow such a thing?! However, when one knows the cultural context out of which the provision comes, it's easier to see the compassion of God at work. Basically, the issue involves a family too poor to bear the cost of a normal wedding. In such a case, a father might "sell" his daughter to a rich man as a "slave." Zilpah and Bilhah (Genesis 29:24, 29) are examples of such "secondary wives." As brides without dowries, they might otherwise have had to contend with exploitation and abuse, but the Law given to Moses on Mount Sinai was aimed at preventing that.

Because it was almost impossible, economically and culturally, for a woman to live independently in those days, she came under the protection of her father before marriage. Then that responsibility passed to the husband. If her husband died, she could return to the protection of her father's household or, if she had an adult son, he was expected to take care of his mother. The last of the commandments provided another protection: other men were not to covet anyone or anything that was part of another man's household (Exodus 20:17). God does not approve of lust and covetousness and wants our hearts filled with holy desires.

However, while women in ancient Israel had many protections and while their position in the nation and in the family was respected (e.g., Ruth 4:11) and the accomplishments of women were sometimes celebrated (Proverbs 31:10–31), the coming of the Savior changed everything for the better.

New Opportunities through Christ

Christ came! His acceptance of and high regard for women of every race and economic status would eventually revolutionize life and culture. "In fact, our Lord's respect and love for all people regardless of their gender, their economic status, their racial heritage, or their personal reputation changed the lives of all His followers forever. The Word had healed them. The Word had brought them help and happy hearts. They couldn't help but follow Him."[28]

Luke's Gospel in particular describes numerous encounters between our Lord and women in villages, towns, cities, and the surrounding countryside. Jesus taught them. He healed them. He forgave them. He often included women as main characters in His parables. He accepted their hospitality and their worship. In turn, many women followed Him. Some of the wealthier women of the day helped support the Lord and His entourage. They stayed with Him as He hung and died on the cross, and they became the first eyewitnesses to His resurrection.[29]

As Jesus traveled around the countryside, He was accompanied not only by the twelve apostles, but also by several women. For everyone in the group, it must have been an amazing and exciting opportunity to learn and to serve—hearing Jesus preach and teach each day, seeing Him heal and perform other miracles, observing His compassion for people with all sorts of needs, continually moving from town to town, watching the crowds grow, and being privileged to personally support His ministry.

Obviously the women who followed Him controlled their own finances and had funds leftover to share. Obviously, too, they had the freedom that following Him demanded. One wonders if they had dropped what they were doing, just as the apostles had. Did they sit at His feet, like Mary of Bethany, trusting that this itinerant rabbi would accept them as His students?

Of the women who traveled with Jesus, Luke identifies three by name in chapter 8 of his Gospel: Mary Magdalene, Joanna, and Susanna. According to verse 2, Jesus had freed each of them from evil spirits and disconcerting diseases. Mary Magdalene's name is placed first here and in six of the other lists in which her name appears in Scripture, indicating the respect the Gospel writers had for her.

With their own finances and possessions, the women in Jesus' retinue probably bought and prepared food; purchased, made, and laundered clothing; and perhaps paid for rooms or beds where Jesus and the Twelve could stay. Few homes of that day were large enough to house a group of thirteen grown men and perhaps a similar number of women. Maybe several families opened their homes in each village the group visited. Maybe they slept in caves in the hillsides or carried bedrolls and slept outdoors most nights. The climate in Israel is warm enough to permit it. Whatever the case, the assistance the women provided was invaluable, and certainly the Lord and the Twelve deeply appreciated it. From these women we learn that supporting the Lord's work involves sharing our time, talent, and financial resources with pastors, missionaries, and other church workers.

What happened to these women?

Susanna is never mentioned again in the Bible; all we know about her is that she followed Jesus and helped support Him.

Joanna was the wife of Chuza, the manager of King Herod's household. His was a responsible position, and the family's wealth likely helped make it possible for Joanna to leave the care of the household in the hands of capable servants. However, considering that Herod was the ruler who beheaded John the Baptist, Joanna must have wondered what could happen if Jesus' teachings similarly angered the king. Like John, Jesus certainly would have condemned Herod for divorcing his first wife and then indulging in an unlawful marriage with Herodias, his brother's wife. Eventually Jesus' activities evidently did provoke Herod, so much so that some of the Pharisees advised Jesus "Get away from here, for Herod wants to kill you" (Luke 13:31).

Scripture does not indicate how much the people in Herod's court knew about Joanna's support for Jesus of Nazareth. How often did she share Jesus' teachings or talk about her experiences while accompanying Him? Obviously her faith and gratitude for her own healing dwarfed any fears she may have had. She, too, used her personal funds to support His ministry, and she remained faithful to the last, even following Jesus to the tomb after His death. The fact that Joanna knew about Jesus shows how fast and how far the news about Him traveled. It quickly influenced even people in high places. Indeed, Jesus came for *all* people.

Because of her name, it is believed that **Mary Magdalene** came from the village of Magdala, about three miles north of Tiberias on the western shore of the Sea of Galilee. Known as the "city of color" in the Talmud, Magdala was home to many people skilled in dyeing woolen cloth. The indigo plant flourished there.[30] A fishing village, its population apparently included numerous prostitutes.

This may be why still today, people wrongly speculate that Mary Magdalene may have been a prostitute. Many prostitutes were single, and Scripture gives no indication that Mary had a husband. If she had been married, she would likely have had the title "Mary, wife of so-and-so." However, early theologians also jumped to the erroneous conclusion that she was the sinful woman brought to Jesus after having been caught in adultery (John 8:3–11). This belief was sealed into the Church's consciousness in AD 591 when Pope Gregory announced in a homily that Mary Magdalene, Mary of Bethany, and the unnamed sinner were the same woman. Not until 1969 did the Catholic Church restore a separate identity to each of them.

Prevalence of Demons

We know from Luke that Jesus cured Mary Magdalene of seven demons. The Gospels cite many examples of demon possession. These include the following:

- *In Luke 11:14, Jesus drove out a demon that was mute. When the demon left, the man who had been mute spoke, and the crowd was amazed.*

- *In Mark 9:17–26, a father brought his deaf and*

mute son, who was apparently also epileptic, to Jesus. Whenever the evil spirit seized the boy, it threw him to the ground, foaming at the mouth, gnashing his teeth, and becoming rigid. Jesus commanded the spirit to come out, and it did, shrieking and violently convulsing the boy.

- In Luke 8:27–36, the Gospel writer describes Jesus' travels through the region of the Gerasenes. Here He encountered a demon-possessed man who wore no clothing and lived in the tombs. (This made him continually "unclean" according to the holiness codes of the Old Testament.) So many demons inhabited this man that they declared their name to be "Legion." When Jesus cast out the demons, they entered a herd of pigs, which immediately rushed down a steep embankment into the lake and drowned.

- Matthew 8:28–32 describes a similar situation, this time with two men. The demons inhabiting these two recognized Jesus as "Son of God." In fact, whenever evil spirits saw Jesus, they fell down before Him and cried out in recognition, "You are the Son of God" (Mark 3:11). This led the "teachers of the law" who came from Jerusalem to investigate. Their conclusion: Jesus had performed the exorcisms in league with Satan (v. 22).

- Matthew 8:16 describes a haunting scene in which twilight is falling. In the semidarkness, many demon-possessed people were brought to Jesus. The Lord ministered in compassion to these tormented individuals, driving out the spirits by His Word and healing the people.

Jesus gave this same power over demonic forces to the seventy-two disciples whom He sent out two by two "ahead of Him . . . into every town and place where He

Himself was about to go" (Luke 10:1). Were some of these disciples women? Scripture does not tell us, but 1 Corinthians 9:5 indicates that the believing wives of Peter and the other apostles and brothers of the Lord did sometimes accompany them.

The seventy-two returned amazed, saying, "Lord, even the demons are subject to us in Your name!" (Luke 10:17). Jesus rejoiced with them, but went on to remind them of a greater joy: "Rejoice that your names are written in heaven" (v. 20). This reminder applies to us today, as our twenty-first-century doctors and scientists, following the Lord's command to subdue the earth (Genesis 1:28), learn to overcome many of the disabling conditions that still plague humanity. Their victories in some cases convince modernists that God is no longer necessary and that demons are not real.

Jesus and His miracles were vividly real to the people who followed Him and especially to Mary Magdalene, who experienced healing firsthand. What were her demons? No one knows. Were the seven the same or different? Were they exorcised at one time or on seven different occasions? Scripture does not say. Some theologians have suggested that because the number seven signifies completion, fullness, and perfection, perhaps the passage means that Mary was totally consumed by them—mentally deranged and unable to function. Regardless, we can only imagine the relief she knew when Christ cured her. Small wonder that she became a devoted follower! We shall meet her again in later chapters, devastated by Jesus' death and rejoicing in His resurrection.

Some religious fiction writers and modern commentators have suggested, based on unauthenticated writings, that Mary Magdalene became Jesus' paramour or wife and even bore Him one or two children. However, Luke's thoroughly researched and well-presented account banishes any unfounded speculation that Jesus and Mary were romantically involved.

Martyrdom

The freedom Christ gave and the compassion He showed made a significant impact on first-century culture. As we said earlier, many women became martyrs in His name.

Details of martyrdom in the first centuries after Christ's ascension are provided in the writings of Tacitus, Eusebius, Tertullian, and other historians. The martyred Perpetua describes her suffering up to the time of her death in her own diary, one of the earliest extant manuscripts by a Christian woman.

Persecution began when Christians refused to worship the Roman emperor as a god. Initially viewed as a sect of Judaism, Christianity spread quickly and without substantial opposition. But before long, followers of Jesus came to be seen as antisocial. They were accused of incest. They were suspected of cannibalism due to a misunderstanding of Holy Communion. They were decried for following a "foreign superstition." According to Tertullian, Christians soon were blamed for every public disaster and every misfortune that befell the people.

Methods of reprisal were so cruel as to be nearly unbelievable. Martyrs, both men and women, were beheaded, weighed down with stones and then tossed into rivers, crucified, burned with hot irons, roasted on grates over fires, and burned at the stake. Their crime? Refusing to deny Christ as Lord and Savior. They went to their deaths willingly, seeing martyrdom as a privilege, an honor, and a victory.[31]

We may think of martyrdom as a thing of the past, but historians tell us that more Christians died or suffered for their faith in the twentieth century than in all the previous nineteen centuries combined. Still today, persecution continues.

Among the early martyrs, the three women most often identified in Christian literature are Blandina, Perpetua, and Felicity.

In AD 177 in Lyons, France (then Gaul), **Blandina,** *a frail young slave, was taken into custody along with her Christian master. After being tortured in numerous ways in an attempt to force her to renounce her faith, Blandina was taken into the amphitheater and bound to a cross-shaped stake to be devoured by wild beasts. It is said that none of the animals touched her. After several beatings, she was taken down and brought back daily to watch the torture of other martyrs. Finally she was thrown in front of a bull, which gored her to death. Observers agreed that no woman had ever been forced to endure so much for so long. Throughout the ordeal, she regularly reminded her torturers, "I am a Christian woman and nothing wicked happens among us."*[32]

In Carthage, North Africa, one of the people imprisoned for her faith about AD 203 was a twenty-two-year-old convert named **Vibia Perpetua.** *She came from a wealthy family and had recently given birth to a son. Perpetua's father pleaded with her to renounce her faith, but she remained steadfast. She was imprisoned with several men and with her slave, Felicity, who was pregnant. The law prohibited the killing of a pregnant woman. Wanting to die with* the others rather than at a later date, Felicity prayed that the baby would be born early. Her prayer was granted two days before the scheduled execution in the Coliseum. Stripped and enmeshed in nets, the women were taken into the arena to face a mad cow. Seeing milk dripping from Felicity's breasts, the crowd objected, so the guards removed the two, clothed them in loose tunics and returned them to the arena to face a gladiator. He effectively dispatched the other prisoners, and then stabbed Perpetua in the ribs. Seeing his hand tremble as he prepared to strike again, Perpetua is said to have grabbed his sword and directed it to her throat. Both Felicity and Perpetua have been considered saints for centuries. A basilica has been erected over their tombs, discovered in 1907.[33]

Catherine of Alexandria died as a martyr in the fourth century. Converting as a teen in Egypt, she rebuked the Roman emperor for persecuting Christians. The emperor sent pagan sages to debate with her, and all fifty were converted to the Christian faith! The emperor then imprisoned Catherine. While she was there, the emperor's soldiers and the empress herself, who visited Catherine, were converted. As a consequence, Catherine was condemned to death on a breaking wheel, a device to which a person was tied spread-eagle and held while an executioner used a large hammer to break all the condemned person's bones. However, tradition says that the wheel broke when Catherine's body touched it, and she was beheaded instead.

When the Protestant Reformation reached England, some women quit attending Mass and were imprisoned and burned at the stake for *refusing to recant.* **Anne Askew** *(1521–1546) said she would rather read five lines in the Bible than attend a Catholic Mass. Anne left a written record with details of her torture, including being placed on a rack that stretched her limbs completely out of their sockets. The torture was intended to get her to incriminate herself and to name others who had similar beliefs. On the day of her execution, she had to be carried to the stake on a chair because she was no longer able to walk.*

Joan Waste *of Derby was blind. Her greatest wish was for a Bible. By helping her father make rope, she saved enough money to buy a Bible. Then she hired a seventy-year-old man in debtors' prison to read to her each day. In this way, she memorized long passages. Because Joan no longer held a Catholic understanding of Holy Communion, she quit going to worship services. For this she was sentenced as a heretic and imprisoned until the pyre could be prepared for her death. She was just twenty-two years old when she died.*

Faith and the Privilege of Mission Work

As the centuries passed, many other faithful people were moved to serve the Lord by sharing their faith at home and abroad.

In the late 1700s, the English became concerned about educating children and teaching the Bible to them, especially the children of working-class people. Most of these children had little or no education, and many of whom, like their parents, worked six days a week in the factories.

One man, **Robert Raikes** *(1735/36–1811), believed that to improve society and decrease the prison population, one must educate the children. In 1780, he hired four women and began classes on Sunday, the only day the children were not working. From 10 a.m. to 2 p.m., the children were taught to read. Then they moved into the church to study the catechism until 5:30 p.m. Some criticized the plan, claiming it defiled the Lord's Day. Some said it was a waste of time to educate "the ragamuffins," and some objected because the teachers were women. But employers saw dramatic changes in the young people, the crime rate dropped, and the Sunday School movement spread.*

One of the first Sunday Schools in the United States was begun in New York in 1816 by **Joanna Bethune** *(1770–1860) and her mother,* **Isabella Graham.** *Initially, 136 students enrolled, and by 1822, the movement included 7,000 students with 600 teachers. Subsequently, the idea of Sunday Schools spread to most Christian denominations.*

Mary Moffat *(1795–1871) and* **Mary Moffat Livingstone** *(1820–1862) served as missionaries in Africa, demonstrating that women could survive life in mud huts with no conveniences, deal with snakes and wild animals, and still witness effectively for Christ. They provided the inspiration for other women to serve in foreign fields.*

Lottie Moon *(1840–1912) went to China as a Southern Baptist missionary. When famine struck there in 1911, she gave away her rations, eating less and less herself, and finally* *died of starvation. Her plea for reinforcements in 1888 launched the first Lottie Moon Christmas offering, which provided three additional missionaries. By the beginning of the 21st century, the Lottie Moon offering was raising more than $150,000,000 annually and supporting over 5,000 missionaries among 1,300 people groups.*

Olive Gruen *(1883–1963) was the first Lutheran Church—Missouri Synod (LCMS) woman commissioned as a missionary. She went to China in 1921, and* **Gertrude Simon,** *a nurse, followed her there in 1926. For several years, Olive served as superintendent of a girls' orphanage at Enshih. In 1939, Enshih became a target in China's war with Japan. Bedding, medicines, and other valuables were moved to Olive's home, giving her a household of sixty in seven rooms and a basement.*

After Gertrude was assigned to the orphanage in 1943, the Japanese invasion forced her, with the help of three staff and several coolies, to transport twenty-two girls more than two hundred miles to safety. The journey took weeks on foot as they carried their charges, including many infants, across a mountain range and a major river. Frequently they camped in caves to escape bombing raids. When both women were forced out of China by Communist policies in 1948, they continued to work among Chinese refugees—Olive in Taiwan and Gertrude in Hong Kong.

Deaconess **Martha Boss,** *a Lutheran nurse, teacher, and evangelist, served as a missionary to China and Hong Kong from 1945 to 1973.*

She invested her life savings in the Lutheran Handicraft Center so refugees coming there might have a means of livelihood.

Alvina Federwitz, *a Lutheran Bible Translator, is typical of many women who have worked to translate the Bible into the spoken languages of people groups around the world. She served with her husband, Rev. Dale Federwitz, in Liberia, West Africa, from 1974 until his death in 2002 and since then has passionately continued efforts to make the Scriptures available in the various heart languages of Liberian people. All four of the Federwitz children have become Bible translators themselves. For her efforts to increase literacy, Alvina was honored by the president of Liberia in July 2007.*

Faith and the Privilege of Serving in Christ's Name

Just as Mary Magdalene, Joanna, and Susanna served Jesus in practical ways, so women through the ages have also served the physical and personal needs of others in His name. In Europe, India, and Africa, several pioneered medical services for women and children, paving the way for modern medical and social ministries. Among those who have served are these:

Macrina *(327–379) was betrothed at age 12, but her fiancé died before their wedding. Macrina then chose a life of perpetual virginity and devoted herself to prayer, meditation, and works of charity. Eventually she formed a community of women in Cappadocia (now Turkey) who shared her Christian goals. After the death of her mother, she raised her ten younger brothers, three of whom became bishops and referred* to her as "The Teacher."

Elizabeth of Hungary *(1207–1231) is said to have worked herself to death for the poor. She was just twenty-three when she died. During the floods and famine of 1226, her husband, Ludwig IV, was in Italy. She assumed control of his affairs, distributing money, opening the royal granaries, and even giving state robes to the poor. She built a hospital and fed nine hundred poor people at the palace gates. She also opened Eastern Europe's first orphanage and personally cared for lepers.*

Dr. **Clara Swain** *(1834–1910) is considered the first female medical missionary in history. She arrived at her destination in India in 1870. Her patient load grew from thirteen hundred the first year to seven thousand a decade later. Women doctors were essential in that culture because males were not allowed to treat women. By 1874, Swain had built the Women's Hospital and Medical School, the first such institution in all of Asia.*

Dr. **Ida S. Scudder** *(1870–1960) also became a medical missionary in India, as were her father and grandfather. Coming from a long line of missionaries (nearly fifty in all with more than eleven hundred combined years of service), Ida nevertheless had no intention of living in India with its famine, poverty, and disease. Educated in the United States, she returned to India when her mother was ill. One day, three men came to the Scudder home at different times, each asking Ida to help his wife, who was having problems giving birth. She offered to send her father, but they rejected that idea because he was a man.*

The next morning, she was shocked to learn that all three women had died. This experience convinced Ida that God was calling her to begin a ministry dedicated to the health needs of the people of India, particularly women and children.[34] *Few medical schools accepted women in those days, but Scudder graduated from Cornell Medical College in 1899, and upon her return to India, founded a clinic in Vellore. Within two years it became a forty-bed hospital, and today it is a seventeen-hundred-bed medical center.*

In 1913, the LCMS sent **Lulu Ellermann,** *R.N., to India to begin medical mission work. She started with a dispensary on the veranda of her bungalow in Bargur. Eventually a doctor was sent also, and Bethesda Hospital was established at Ambur. Later,* **Angela Rehwinkel***, the facility's nursing supervisor, became the glue that held the hospital together as doctor after doctor came and went. Rehwinkel served in India from 1920 to 1959, retiring at age 76.*

Mission Groups Provide Support

Today, thousands of women serve as both long-term and short-term missionaries around the world. Since the early 1800s, many of them have been supported by women's missionary organizations in most major Christian denominations. Members are committed to praying, raising funds, and encouraging personnel in the mission field.

That same dedication to service is embodied in the deaconess movement, begun in Europe in the early 1800s and launched in the United States in 1850. Its purpose is described by the motto adopted by the Concordia Deaconess Conference: "Working in faith, laboring in love, remaining steadfast in the hope of our Lord Jesus Christ."

Employed in various positions in churches, schools, missions, and service organizations around the world, today's deaconesses share the Gospel of Jesus Christ as they perform works of mercy, provide spiritual care, and teach the Christian faith.

"Working in faith and laboring in love" also describes the attitude of the delegates attending the organizing convention of the Lutheran Women's Missionary League in 1942 in Chicago. After adopting a constitution and choosing a name for the new auxiliary, they proceeded to elect officers. Several nominees were apprehensive about their ability to handle such a large responsibility and asked to have their names withdrawn from the ballot.

Finally, Rev. Oscar Fedder, one of the pastoral advisors appointed by the church body, stood up and said, "When the Lord taps you on the shoulder and says, 'I need you for this job,' you must not turn Him down. If He thought you were incapable, He would not have chosen you."

While Jesus physically walked here on earth, He welcomed and encouraged women to serve Him and His disciples. Jesus included women as He taught, and He healed their physical afflictions. Most important, He forgave their sins. Their response was to serve Him and make it easier for His apostles to fulfill their call to ministry in His name.

Still today, Jesus welcomes women into His family: "Whoever does the will of God, he is My brother and sister and mother" (Mark 3:35). He assures us that if we call upon the name of the Lord, we will be saved (Acts 2:21). He promises that His Spirit will be poured out on both men and women (Acts 2:18). And He calls each of us to use our gifts to reach out in mercy, mission, and service to all who are in need of His saving message. He welcomes and encourages us. He teaches and He heals. He forgives. He saves. To Him be the glory!

The Heart of Jesus as Shown in the Lives of Mary Magdalene, Joanna, and Susanna

Because of Jesus' amazing counter-cultural acceptance of women and through His recognition and use of their talents and abilities, women today are motivated to use their God-given gifts to further His Church and share His Good News.

The Dead Girl and the Sick Woman

Recovered Daughter, Suffering Believer
Luke 8:40–56; Matthew 9:18–26; Mark 5:21–43

There came a man named Jairus, who was a ruler of the synagogue. And falling at Jesus' feet, he implored Him to come to his house, for he had an only daughter, about twelve years of age, and she was dying. . . . When He came to the house, . . . [all the people] laughed at Him, knowing that she was dead. But taking her by the hand He called, saying, "Child, arise." And her spirit returned, and she got up at once. Luke 8:41–42, 51a, 53–55

And there was a woman who had had a discharge of blood for twelve years, and . . . she could not be healed by anyone. She came up behind Him and touched the fringe of His garment, and im-

*mediately her discharge of blood ceased. And
Jesus said, "Who was it that touched Me?" .
. . When the woman saw that she was not hid-
den, she came trembling and [fell] down before
Him. . . . He said to her, "Daughter, your faith
has made you well; go in peace." Luke 8:43–45,
47–48*

The two intertwined narratives in Luke 8 provide an
amazing study in contrasts. Consider:

- *The young girl whom Jesus raised from the dead
  had grown up in a prominent, respected family. The
  woman He healed was a social outcast; the whole
  town knew she was unclean!*

- *The daughter of Jairus had an influential father to
  plead with Jesus on her behalf. The woman with the
  flow of blood was alone, perpetually unclean, and
  therefore possibly estranged from her family. She had
  to struggle through the jostling crowd by herself.*

- *The girl had lived twelve years in comfort and now
  looked forward to marriage, menstruation, and a
  family of her own. The woman had struggled for
  twelve years because of the laws related to blood and
  desperately wanted to be healed. Mark tells us that
  she had "suffered much under many physicians, and
  had spent all that she had, and was no better but
  rather grew worse" (Mark 5:26).*

Doctors and Medicine

Luke was a physician. How we wish he had been
more specific regarding the treatments the woman had
undergone. What did the doctors prescribe that caused
more suffering? We can only guess based on what we know
about medical practice in the first century.

Physicians were few in number in those centuries and are rarely mentioned in Scripture. Historians believe that most physicians lacked training and often relied on "magical" potions and superstitions. However, some may have practiced surgery. Archaeologists have discovered knives, saws, tweezers, forceps, chisels, and scoops dating to 1500 BC and beyond.[35] Some physicians also practiced bloodletting,[36] and skeletons have been found with holes drilled in their skulls. Job called his friends "worthless physicians" (Job 13:4). In Greco-Roman culture, Asclepius was worshiped as the god of healing. His temples contained numerous spas where people bathed, rested, enjoyed massages, and ate a diet that included popular herbs and "medicines" of that day.

It is believed that the first medicines came from Egypt. Ingredients included minerals, herbs, wines, fruits, and other parts of plants. Mixtures of wine, oil, and herbs were often used to anoint people.

When Jesus sent the disciples out two by two, they anointed many sick people with oil and healed them (Mark 6:13). In Luke 10:34, the Good Samaritan poured oil and wine on the injured man's wounds and bandaged them. Oil was also used for scalp diseases and was believed to kill lice.

Physicians are seldom mentioned in Scripture, most likely because the Israelites believed that illness was a result of sin, and they depended primarily on the Lord for healing. When they left Egypt, the Lord told them explicitly: "If you will diligently listen to the voice of the LORD your God, and do that which is right in His eyes, and give ear to His commandments and keep all His statutes, I will put none of the diseases on you that I put on the Egyptians, for I am the LORD, your healer" (Exodus 15:26).

The Law of Moses delegated various diagnostic

and healing tasks to the priests. When anyone had a skin disease, for example, they were to be brought to the priest (Leviticus 13:2–3). When Asa, king of Judah, developed a serious foot disease, he went to the physicians instead of to the Lord for a cure. The writer of Chronicles criticizes him for this (2 Chronicles 16:12). Psalm 103:2–3 affirms the power and willingness of the Lord to heal His people: "Bless the LORD, O my soul, and forget not all His benefits, who forgives all your iniquity, who heals all your diseases."

Made Well by Faith

Whatever procedures her doctors had tried, the woman of Luke 8 seized her opportunity when Jesus arrived in her village. No doubt she had heard about the many people He had healed. Now was her chance—she would go to Him for her cure! He arrived by boat on the west side of Lake Galilee. Edging her way through the crowd that greeted Him, she made her way along behind Him. Full of faith, she kept thinking, *if only I can touch His clothes, I will be made well.*

Then, success! She touched one of the tassels of His garment! Jewish men were required under the Law to wear an outer garment with tassels on the four corners to remind them to follow God's Ten Commandments (Numbers 15:38–40). Their garments sometimes billowed like wings. In Jesus' case, this would have brought to mind the promise of Malachi 4:2: "The sun of righteousness shall rise with healing in its wings."

Immediately upon touching the tassel, the woman was healed! The hemorrhaging that had plagued her for twelve years stopped in an instant. After years of expensive treatments, just one touch, motivated by faith in Him, did it! No longer would the chairs she sat on, the bed she slept on, and everything she touched be unclean. No longer would anyone who touched her or her chair or her bed be unclean. No longer would she be a pitiable outcast, restricted from the nation's public worship. All she wanted to do now was slip away to the temple to make the required sacrifice (two doves or young pigeons, one for a sin offering and one for a burnt offering), and thus obtain ritual purification.

Suddenly she saw it wasn't going to be that easy. Jesus had felt power go out from Him. Now He was asking, "Who touched My clothes?"

The disciples thought the question ridiculous. They were surrounded, even crushed, by the large crowd. Everyone was jostling against Him, wanting to be as close as possible to Him. "Someone did touch Me!" Jesus insisted, explaining that He felt power go out from His body. But this wasn't an accusation; it was an invitation for the woman to come forward. Jesus would use her touch to teach.

The woman realized she could no longer remain anonymous. She had to confess. Trembling with fear, she moved forward. Would He be angry? Her touch had made Him unclean. Most Jewish teachers avoided women in public. What would He say or do?

Bowing before Him and in front of all the people, she told the whole truth. She described her plight, her chronic bleeding, her need for healing, and the joyful result the touch had brought. How relieved she must have felt when she heard His words: "Daughter, your faith has made you well; go in peace, and be healed of your disease" (Mark 5:34).

He called her "daughter"! Her own family may have deserted her because her uncleanness contaminated everything she touched, making it almost impossible to live with her. But now Jesus included her, healed her, acknowledged her faith, cared about her. And, by compassionately healing her affliction, He erased her shame and fear.

In those amazing words, Jesus also showed that His perfect life, lived on our behalf, fulfilled all the ritualistic laws and ceremonies required by the old covenant given on Mount Sinai. Quite apart from making any animal sacrifice or going through any purification ritual, she was clean! Similarly, our Lord's own blood, shed on the cross, would secure forgiveness of sins for all repentant believers without any sacrifice or ritualistic service on our part.

Recognizing the compassion Jesus showed to the woman, we can openly and without shame approach Him for healing and forgiveness. His gentleness in relating to her provides additional proof of His concern for us, His "sisters" in the family of God. This incident, relating as it does to menstruation, is specific to women; no man could receive the same healing.

An Unappreciated Interruption

For Jairus, of course, this healing represented an interruption. His daughter lay dying. How could Jesus pause to deal with an unclean woman when He was on such an important mission? The question must have run through Jairus's head. His urgency knew no bounds. Jesus had to arrive at his daughter's bedside before it was too late!

As a leader in the synagogue, most likely the synagogue Jesus Himself attended when He found Himself near Capernaum, Jairus was used to having people act immediately when he made requests. When he met Jesus, Jairus had not simply asked for help. He had knelt at the Lord's feet and earnestly pleaded with the miracle worker to come to his home. Unlike many other Jewish leaders, Jairus sincerely believed in Jesus' power. If Jesus would lay

His hands on her, his daughter would be made well and live. How relieved this concerned father must have been when Jesus agreed to come, to help.

But then came the unexpected interruption by the bleeding woman. Worse yet, while Jesus was still talking with the woman, some messengers came from Jairus's home with news no father ever wants hear. The messengers said, in essence, "Your daughter is dead. There's no longer any reason for you to go on inconveniencing the Teacher."

Dead! What finality that word carries. Life here on earth has ended. No more sharing, talking, hugging. No more dreaming, envisioning the future. For the girl, no marriage, no giving birth to children. For her parents, no grandchildren, no future generations through her.

How shocked Jairus must have been when Jesus paid no attention to this news. Instead, Jesus said, "Don't be afraid! Only believe, and she will get well." Taking only Peter, James, and John with Him, Jesus moved on to Jairus's home. Already the mourners were there with their flutes (a favored instrument for this situation, continuing the custom of Jeremiah 48:36). This was not just a coma; the girl was dead, and they all knew it. They were weeping, wailing loudly, and beating their breasts. Just as with the son of the widow of Nain, the sequence of events moved rapidly after death occurred in that hot climate. The burial would happen within the next twenty-four hours due to the rapid decomposition that began to occur immediately.

All the mourners laughed in derision at Jesus when He asked, "Why are you making a commotion and weeping? The child is not dead but sleeping" (Mark 5:39). Then, shooing everyone out of the room except the three disciples and the girl's parents, Jesus took the child's hand, becoming ritually contaminated for the second time that day, this time by touching a dead person.

As He touched her, He called out, "Talitha cumi" (v. 41). This Aramaic command meant "Little girl, I tell you, wake up!" Scholars emphasize that the term *little girl* indicates affection and His words could also be translated "Little lamb, get up!" Jesus was addressing her by a term of endearment; He was calling her "My little lamb."

Immediately the child's spirit returned; she began walking around. Imagine her parents' amazement and joy! At that moment, Jesus became the practical one, addressing the girl's physical needs by suggesting that someone find something for her to eat. He also directed them not to tell anyone—but, of course, news of a miracle like this was bound to spread.

Eight Restorations

Word doubtless spread just as rapidly and widely as did news of the other biblical miracles in which God restored life to a corpse. Besides the resurrection of Christ, Scripture tells us of eight dead people who were brought back to life. In addition to Jairus's daughter, these miracles include:

- **The son of the widow of Nain.** *Chapter 4 of this book describes this miracle in detail.*

- **The son of the widow of Zarephath** *(1 Kings 17:17–24). When drought hit Israel (the Northern Kingdom), the Lord sent Elijah the prophet to Zarephath in Sidon to the home of a widow, telling him she would care for him. As mentioned in chapter 4, Elijah asked for water, then for a piece of bread. The widow had neither—only a handful of flour and a little oil. She intended to make one final meal for herself and her son; they would eat it and then resign themselves to death by starvation. At Elijah's* request, she made a small loaf of bread for him. The Lord blessed both it and her. Amazingly, her supply of flour and oil did not run out from that moment until the famine ended. However, some time later, the son became ill and died. The widow was devastated. Elijah prayed that the boy's life would be restored, and the Lord answered his prayer.

- **The son of the Shunammite woman** (2 Kings 4:32–37). When Elisha stopped in Shunem one day, a wealthy woman recognized him as a man of God and invited him to her home. Graciously she suggested to her husband that they make a small room for Elisha and his servant Gehazi on the roof of their home. They would furnish it with a bed, table, chair, and lamp so he could stay there whenever he came through their town. Their home undoubtedly had a flat roof like others of that time, so the project was not difficult. (How different it would be for us to do this today—we'd need architect's drawings, building permits, a contractor, roofer, plumber, electrician, painter, building inspector, and much more!)

  Wanting to do something for the couple in return, Elisha asked the Lord to provide this childless, elderly couple with a child. Sure enough, the wife became pregnant and gave birth to a son. However, when the child was a few years old, he developed a tremendous headache and died just a few hours later. Quickly the woman saddled a donkey and rode off to find Elisha, who was at Mount Carmel. At her urgent request, Elisha returned to her home and prostrated himself on the boy until his body grew warm. The boy sneezed seven times and opened his eyes. His life was restored!

- **A dead man** (2 Kings 13:20–21). As some Israelites were burying a man, they saw Moabite raiders

approaching. In their rush to escape, they quickly threw the body into the tomb of Elisha, who had died some time previously. When the body "touched the bones of Elisha, [the man] revived and stood on his feet."

- **Lazarus** *(John 11:1–44). We will discuss this miracle in detail in chapter 8.*

- **Dorcas** *(Acts 9:36–42). A disciple who was always doing good and helping poor people, Dorcas was deeply loved by all who knew her. When she became sick and died, her friends sent for Peter, who was nearby in Lydda. "Please come at once," they urged. Upon his arrival, all the widows who had benefited from her care and sewing stood around, weeping. They showed Peter many of the robes and other clothing Dorcas had made for them. Sending them all out of the room where her body was, Peter knelt and prayed. Then he said, "Tabitha, get up," and she did. As he helped her to her feet, Peter called the others and presented her to them, alive. The result: Many believed! Many women's mission and ministry societies have been named in memory of Dorcas. The members strive to follow her example of caring for the poor and needy.*

- **Eutychus** *(Acts 20:7–12). When Paul stopped off in Troas briefly, he joined the believers in a meal and in the Lord's Supper ("breaking bread"). Since he intended to leave the next day and since he had much to tell them and much instruction to share, he continued talking with them until midnight! Undoubtedly the room grew muggy in the warm climate. In addition, many lamps were likely burning, absorbing the oxygen and making the room very stuffy. A young man named Eutychus, seated on the sill of an open window in the crowded third story room,* *became groggy and soon fell fast asleep. Tragically, he lost his balance and fell to the ground. Rushing down to pick him up, the believers realized he was dead. Paul threw himself on the body, put his arms around him, and assured the people, "Don't be alarmed—he's alive!" Much to their surprise, he was! The assemblage returned upstairs, talked until daylight, and then took Eutychus home. All felt greatly comforted.*

Blood and Menstruation

In each of these eight cases, we see the impotence of death in the face of our Lord's mercy and power. We can assume that Jairus's daughter did reach maturity and, like other women of her day, had to deal with menstruation, laws related to blood, and the Mosaic Law rules regarding uncleanness.

Leviticus 15:18–33 includes a series of regulations regarding the impurity resulting from menstruation or a continuing discharge such as the sick woman experienced. The "holiness codes" given under the old covenant, the covenant of Sinai, also included regulations relating to normal sexual activity. However, ordinary menstruation and intercourse with the opposite sex did not require sacrifices for purification—only a ritual washing afterward.

The regulations concerning menstruation included a seven-day period of uncleanness (probably based on a normal five-day flow plus two extra days in the event it lasted slightly longer). When David first saw Bathsheba from the roof of his palace, she was bathing to cleanse herself from her monthly period (2 Samuel 11:2, 4).

The time of uncleanness included other inconvenient consequences, as Leviticus 15:19–24 indicates:

Whoever touches [a menstruating woman] shall be unclean until the evening. And everything on which she lies during her menstrual impurity shall be unclean. Everything also on which she sits shall be unclean. And whoever touches her bed shall wash his clothes and bathe himself in water and be unclean until the evening. And whoever touches anything on which she sits shall wash his clothes and bathe himself in water and be unclean until the evening. . . . And if any man lies with her and her menstrual impurity comes upon him, he shall be unclean seven days, and every bed on which he lies shall be unclean.

While this may seem to make "normal life" impossible, we need to remember that compared with women in Western societies today, Israelite women menstruated much less often. For one thing, most bore many children. Menstruation, of course, stops during pregnancy and is rare during breastfeeding. Regular menstrual periods were not as common then as now.[37]

Moreover, not only the women but also the men had to deal with impurity laws. According to Leviticus 15:1–12, 16–18, men who experienced a seminal discharge had to follow a cleansing ritual similar to the cleansing women performed following their period. They washed their clothes and bathed. A seminal discharge made them "unclean," and it made any bed, chair, or saddle on which they sat unclean as well. Unless they rinsed their hands first, they passed on the "uncleanness" to anyone they touched. Any pottery an unclean man touched had to be broken, and any wooden vessel he used had to be ritually cleansed. If a man and woman came together and some sperm spilled, they both had to take a bath and were unclean until evening. Interestingly, if a man with any discharge spit on a clean person, the same cleansing procedures had to be followed by the clean person. As those who tried to obey all these regulations soon discovered, it was impossible to do so perfectly.[38] Some of these laws are similar to universal precautions practiced today in the health care industry.

The word *blood* appears about three hundred times in the Old Testament, usually in conjunction with the blood of temple sacrifices, and about ninety times in the New, generally in relation to the saving blood of Christ. With such strong and repeated emphasis on blood and its regulation, we need to ask what purpose was served by the Old Testament laws and rituals, especially those that focused on blood.

Obviously there were sanitary components to the Lord's directives in an era when little was understood about the spread of disease. More important, however, the holiness code provisions that focused on blood served as a kind of object lesson about human sin and the holiness of God and the provision He would make to deal with human sin through the blood of Christ.

From observation, the people realized that when a body bleeds extensively, the person may die. Likewise, because we sin, we have all incurred the penalty for sin: death. As Scripture says, "The soul who sins shall die" (Ezekiel 18:20), and "For the wages of sin is death, but the free gift of God is eternal life in Christ Jesus our Lord" (Romans 6:23).

God's Plan: Send a Savior

Our perfect God demands perfection, and we are not perfect. Our holy God demands holiness, and we are not holy. Unholy people who encounter holiness find themselves destroyed by it. In Isaiah 6, the prophet finds himself suddenly swept up in a vision into the presence of God and exclaims, in essence, "I'm a dead man! My eyes have seen the King, the Lord of Glory!" (v. 5). Yet, despite our sinfulness, our unholiness, our Lord loves us still. He loves us so much that He wants us to enjoy serving Him here on earth and then join Him to live with Him forever in the glories of His holy, heavenly home!

To make this possible, our just and merciful Lord came up with a plan that He set in motion at the moment sin entered the world. Over and over in the Old Testament, we find the promise and details of that plan. Throughout the New Testament, we see those promises fulfilled. Here are just a few examples:

- *Genesis 3:15 promises that a descendant of Eve will crush Satan's head (NIV).*

- *Passages in Genesis assure Abraham that "in you" (12:3) and "in your offspring" (22:18) would all nations of the earth be blessed. The Savior would arrive in the lineage of Abraham who would be called to faith by his faithful Lord and made righteous through that faith.*

- *Psalm 22 as a whole describes our Lord's crucifixion in detail, including the fact that the soldiers would gamble over His clothing (v. 18)—this around a thousand years before it occurred and centuries before crucifixion as a form of execution was invented!*

- *Isaiah 7:14 foretells our Lord's virgin birth: "The virgin shall conceive and bear a son, and shall call His name Immanuel."*

- *Isaiah 9:6 adds that the child will be called "Wonderful Counselor, Mighty God, Everlasting Father, Prince of Peace."*

- *Micah 5:2 adds that the Savior would be born in Bethlehem.*

- *Malachi 3:1 describes the messenger who would serve as a forerunner for the Christ; it fits the ministry of John the Baptizer to the last detail.*

- *Isaiah 53:4–5 offers the comforting reassurance that God's Servant would be "wounded for our trans-gressions" and "crushed for our iniquities." Truly, "with His stripes we are healed."*

Yes, through Christ, we are saved and healed eternally. No longer are the blood rituals of the Old Testament necessary. Since in our spiritual, dead condition, we could never hope to pay for our sins ourselves (Ephesians 2:1); since the blood of goats and calves could never remove sin (Hebrews 10:4); and since our God loved us with an everlasting love (Jeremiah 31:3), He sent His perfect Son to shed His blood for us at Calvary (Romans 5:8–9; Titus 3:5–7).

However, until Christ appeared on earth, the Mosaic Law directed that the blood of certain animals be shed vicariously for those who were sorry for what they had done and trusted in God's promise to send the Savior. Those animals had to be spotless and perfect, for they pointed toward the great, perfect, final sacrifice that would be made by Christ.

We today recall what Christ did for us on the cross whenever we partake of Holy Communion. But this Meal is more than simply a memorial. Paul writes: "The cup of blessing that we bless, is it not a participation in the blood of Christ? The bread that we break, is it not a participation in the body of Christ?" (1 Corinthians 10:16). In a very real way, the Lord's Supper is God's word of reconciliation and redemption in visible form. There we receive the very body and blood our Savior gave and shed for us on His cross. Our Friend has paid our ransom, and we go free—free from sin, free from shame, free from guilt.

How thankful we can be that Christ's sacrifice abolished the bloody system of animal sacrifice forever. How wonderful that in its place, we can worship our crucified and risen Savior through all eternity. As Hebrews 9:12–14 assures us:

> *He entered once for all into the holy places, not by means of the blood of goats and calves but by means of His own blood, thus securing an eternal redemption. For if the blood of goats and bulls, and the sprinkling of defiled persons with the ashes of a heifer, sanctify for the purification of the flesh, how much more will the blood of Christ, who through the eternal Spirit offered Himself without blemish to God, purify our conscience from dead works to serve the living God.*

Forgiven, healed, and restored to new life, Jairus's daughter could serve. Made clean, the sick woman could rejoice in her new life and live to serve her merciful Savior by serving His people. Forgiven and healed from the terminal illness that is sin, we, too, have received God's gift of new life. We, too, are free to serve, encouraged and enabled to use the talents our Lord gives us to serve His purposes wherever and whenever He calls us.

The Heart of Jesus as Shown in the Lives of the Dead Girl and the Sick Woman

Whether we are young, old, or something in between, God loves, forgives, prepares, and enables us as His daughters to serve Him. He promises each of us an eternal home in heaven with Him when our service on this earth ends.

Martha and Mary

Conscientious Hostess, Serious Student

Luke 10:38–42

Now as they went on their way, Jesus entered a village. And a woman named Martha welcomed Him into her house. And she had a sister called Mary, who sat at the Lord's feet and listened to His teaching. But Martha was distracted with much serving. And she went up to Him and said, "Lord, do you not care that my sister has left me to serve alone? Tell her then to help me." But the Lord answered her, "Martha, Martha, you are anxious and troubled about many things, but one thing is necessary. Mary has chosen the good portion, which will not be taken away from her." Luke 10:38–42

Imagine having a dozen or more important guests drop in unexpectedly! How would you cope? If you had to prepare dinner, could you do it all alone?

That was Martha's predicament when she graciously opened her home to Jesus and His disciples. As we have seen, Jesus' entourage included women in addition to the Twelve. Who knows how many other followers tagged along on this occasion! The number easily could have been more than a dozen. Some Bible scholars believe Martha's household was a wealthy one and may have included servants. Martha may have sent the invitation to Jesus and His followers in advance. Even so, once guests began to arrive, the primary responsibility for showing hospitality and for preparing and serving food fell to the women of the household. In this case, that included Martha and Mary.

It is interesting that Jesus sent out the Twelve (Luke 9:1–5) and the seventy-two (Luke 10:1–7) without purse or provisions. People who received them would provide for them, He explained. Likewise on His own journeys to spread the Gospel of the kingdom of God, He Himself depended on the generosity of those to whom He ministered. Seemingly, Martha intended to model what Jesus anticipated and instructed.

Of course, we cannot tell from the text how many guests arrived with Jesus, and it doesn't matter. Even if He had been the only guest, Martha still would have wanted everything done perfectly. She wanted to honor Him. From the text we can guess that Martha not only loved the Lord, but she also loved entertaining and was good at it—but she needed help.

Preparing a meal just wasn't that easy in those days before freezers, refrigerators, microwaves, gas and electric ovens, toasters, grills, running water, and packaged foods. Nor could they visit a nearby twenty-four-hour store where supplies and ready-to-serve items were readily available. No, every hand, every helper was essential for this dinner party's preparation.

Complicating the matter of food preparation was the necessity of doing everything from scratch, including raising, bartering for, or catching every ingredient. Then there were all the Mosaic Laws regarding clean and unclean meat, fish, and fowl that must be observed. No wonder Martha's head was spinning! No wonder she was upset that Mary was doing something unacceptable for a woman in that day—sitting at a rabbi's feet and learning. Didn't Mary realize what had to be done to honor this special guest![39]

Scripture does not tell us how Martha responded to Jesus' admonishment about choosing the "one thing needed." Did she join Mary and learn alongside her at Jesus' feet? (In John 11, we see that Martha had developed strong faith.) As Jesus finished His teaching for the day, did both women return to their work as hostesses? Scripture doesn't tell us. But the questions are interesting!

Bread Making—A Daily Task

Bread was an every-meal basic.[40] Women baked it every day, day after day, because it molded quickly in the hot climate of Palestine, especially in summer. In addition, the small ovens of the time made it almost impossible to bake several loaves of the size we bake today. All this gives new meaning to the Fourth Petition of the Lord's Prayer, "Give us this day our daily bread."

The baking process did not begin with pulling a canister of flour from the shelf. First, the grain (generally wheat or barley) had to be ground. In this agrarian society, the grain usually came from the family's fields. Grinding took so much time that morning, noon, evening, and sometimes after sundown, one could hear the hum of the grinding wheel in most Israelite homes and villages.

The most efficient handmills were operated by two people working together. They consisted of two round stones, eighteen to twenty-four inches in diameter and six inches thick, one on top of the other, with a pivot in the center. The stones were placed on a sheepskin that caught the ground meal or flour. The upper stone had a hole in the middle into which the raw grain was thrown. It also had a handle, or possibly two, which were pushed or pulled to make the top wheel turn—and thus, grind.

If one woman were working alone, she might simply place the grain in a hollowed-out stone and pound it with another stone. Obviously, that took much longer. To get fine flour, the meal was sifted through a sieve made of rushes and papyrus. Anything remaining in the sieve would be ground again.

Next, the flour, water, and oil were placed in a wooden bowl, kneaded, and then baked. Sometimes families would save a bit of the dough from the day before to serve as a kind of "starter leaven," but mostly they ate unleavened flat bread.

Some towns had semipublic ovens or even a public baker who baked the dough for purchase; Jeremiah 37:21 mentions a bakers' street. However, most women did their own baking using various types of ovens. We wouldn't appreciate any of them. The simplest was a large earthenware jar in which the woman started a fire of grass, stubble, and twigs. When it was hot enough, round, thin pieces of dough were plastered on the outside of the jar where they baked quickly. Some families dug a pit in the earth, laid flat stones in the bottom, and built a fire over them. When the stones were hot, the fire and ashes were removed and the dough was placed on the stones to bake. Wealthier families had hearths or portable ovens.

Also on the Menu?

Meals often included milk and honey. As God had said, the Promised Land flowed with milk and honey (Exodus 3:8)—but people still had to deal with the bees and milking. Honey was used for sweetening.[41] "Milk" rarely meant cow's milk, but usually that of sheep or goats (Deuteronomy 32:14). Several Scripture passages mention butter and cheese, but these may have differed from the foods we enjoy today, perhaps being simply coagulated milk made by pouring the liquid into a skin sack and shaking (churning) it until it curdled.

Normally, olive oil was spread on bread and used in cooking. Olives were an important staple. The Israelite people ate them as food, pickled them, and pressed them to obtain the oil, which they also used for anointing, skin care, preserving, and medicinal purposes. It kept for years.

Their vegetables were mostly beans and lentils, although Isaiah 1:8 mentions a cucumber field. Esau sold his birthright for a meal of lentils and bread (Genesis 25:29–34). When they were taken to Babylon as captives, Daniel and his three friends requested permission to consume only vegetables and water rather than the rich food and wine of the king (Daniel 1:12). They remained healthy and strong on that diet, and they avoided the guilt that would have been associated with eating food that had first been offered ritualistically to the Babylonian idols. (See 1 Corinthians 8.)

As for meat, Leviticus 11 gives very specific directions: The animals God allowed the Israelites to eat had to chew their cud and have completely divided, split hoofs. This left out pigs, rabbits, and camels. Before eating the flesh of any clean animal, the blood had to be drained because the "blood is its life" (Leviticus 17:14). Orthodox Jews still adhere to this practice today, using only kosher meats and following the food-preparation rules of the Torah.

The people did not eat meat every day. When they did prepare meat as a main dish, they most often prepared goat or lamb. These were roasted or boiled in water or milk. Calf (veal) was considered the most festive and was reserved for special occasions; Jesus' parable of the prodigal son illustrates this (Luke 15:23). God prohibited eating most fowl, but partridges, quail, geese, and pigeons were allowed under the covenant of Sinai.

Similarly, faithful Israelites could eat only fish with fins and scales. Because of the proximity of the Jordan River and the Sea of Galilee, fish were readily available. Jesus prepared a breakfast of bread and fish for His disciples (John 21:12), and He fed a crowd of five thousand with five loaves and two fish (Matthew 14:13–21). He also fed four thousand men, plus women and children, with seven loaves and a few small fish (Matthew 15:32–38; Mark 8:1–9). After He rose from the dead, Jesus ate a piece of broiled fish to prove to the doubting disciples that He was not a ghost (Luke 24:42–43).

Meats and breads were often seasoned with spices: mustard, capers, cumin, saffron, coriander, cinnamon, mint, dill, garlic, onions—and the daily essential, salt. Fruits, when available, gave balance to the diet: figs, grapes, pomegranates, apricots, and dates. Some fruits, especially grapes, were dried and pressed into cakes for storage and trade. The Israelites also enjoyed walnuts, almonds, and pistachios. They drank water, milk, fermented juices, and especially wine, which was usually diluted with water.

Doesn't all this make you wonder what Martha had on her menu the day Jesus came to dinner? Poor people often existed on little more than barley bread, olives, fruit, and locusts, using salt as a dressing. Martha probably served much more elaborate fare!

As we think about Martha's dinner party, we might find ourselves wondering where she planned to serve it. Homes of that period rarely had dining rooms, and people often ate in open-air courtyards. They would sit cross-legged on the ground around an animal skin or cloth—something like a picnic blanket. Some large homes of wealthy people had benches or a space where guests could recline around low tables arranged in a U-shape.

Utensils were rudimentary. Most families had flint knives for cutting meat and fruit, but spoons and forks are not mentioned in the literature of that time. Some scholars speculate that shells may have served as spoons. Many families had flat, broad, metal cups for dipping into the stew pot, but often, too, a piece of bread would be folded and used as a sop for this purpose. Sometimes the master of the house dipped the sops and gave them to his guests. Otherwise, each person dipped into the pot in turn. During the Last Supper, Judas rudely dipped his bread into the dish at the same time as Jesus, who used this incident to identify Judas as the one who would betray Him (Matthew 26:23).

Bread was never cut—it was "broken" (Matthew 26:26; Luke 24:35; Acts 20:11). Apparently, since bread was a staple of life, cutting bread was seen as cutting life itself. Jesus applied this analogy to Himself when He said, "I am the bread of life" (John 6:35).

The Israelites normally ate only two meals a day—breakfast (sometime between 9 a.m. and noon) and dinner in the evening. Tradition also required faithful Jews to wash their hands in a ceremonial way before eating (Matthew 15:2; Mark 7:1–3). On at least one occasion, when the Lord's disciples failed to follow this tradition prescribed by the rabbis, the Pharisees became very upset. Jesus respond-

ed by calling them hypocrites and quoting the prophet
Isaiah:

> *This people draw near with their*
> *mouth and honor Me with their lips,*
> *while their hearts are far from Me,*
> *and their fear of Me is a*
> *commandment taught by men.*

> *Isaiah 29:13*

Jesus continued: "You leave the commandment of God
and hold to the tradition of men" (Mark 7:8).

The traditions of that day also held that women were
to tend to the home, making sure everyone was fed and
clothed, while men usually dealt with matters of providing for the family and teaching the faith. The Law of Moses
did not require women to participate in the major Jewish
religious festivals—the Feast of Weeks, Feast of Unleavened Bread, and Feast of Tabernacles (Deuteronomy 16:16;
Exodus 23:17), but most of them did.

Women Encouraged to Learn

As Christ ministered in Judea and Galilee, little by
little, He changed just about everything for women! He
allowed women to follow Him, and in Bethany, He welcomed Mary's interest in listening to and learning from
Him. He approved her priority in response to Martha's
urgent plea: "Lord, do You not care that my sister has left
me to serve alone? Tell her then to help me" (Luke 10:40).

Martha wanted to do her best for Jesus. But Jesus
wanted what was best for Martha. His answer was compassionate and caring: "Martha, Martha, you are anxious
and troubled about many things, but one thing is necessary. Mary has chosen the good portion, which will not be

taken away from her." This answer continues to bless all women still today; it approves and encourages our study of Christ's message and mission. Jesus came to see Mary, Martha, and Lazarus to discuss, to teach, and to educate—not to be entertained—and He welcomed Mary as a full participant in the process. Jesus' answer encourages us in the God-given desire to grow spiritually and in our knowledge and understanding of God's will.

Martha wanted to serve a meal worthy of her honored guest! That took attention to details. It took time and work. For Martha, there was no time to chat! Yet, she felt comfortable enough in the presence of her guest to be honest with Him and freely share her worries.

Jesus' answer probably surprised her. "Only one thing is needed," He explained. Mary discovered it, and "it will not be taken away from her" (v. 42 NIV). For believers in every era, only one thing is ultimately important: learning, knowing, understanding, and believing God's love for us in Jesus Christ. This thing will not—*must* not—be taken away from Mary or from any one of us. The New Testament writers emphasize this principle again and again:

- *Every believer, every man, woman, and child is to "grow in the grace and knowledge of our Lord and Savior Jesus Christ" (2 Peter 3:18).*

- *Through Christ, "the whole body, joined and held together by every joint with which it is equipped," is to grow and build itself up "in love" as each part does its work (Ephesians 4:16).*

- *Like newborn babies, each one of us is to "long for the pure spiritual milk, that by it [we] may grow up into [our] salvation" (1 Peter 2:2).*

In those days, most women could not read. There were no books as we now know them—only the scrolls of the Old Testament and the writings of historians. Only a very few families or individuals owned such scrolls. (During his service to the king of Babylon when Israel was in exile, Daniel had a copy of the Book of Jeremiah [Daniel 9:2].) Most religious teaching was done orally by learned rabbis in the synagogues and by fathers in their homes.

How blessed we are today! Most people learn to read. Almost every Christian home has at least one copy of the Bible, and most of us own several versions. Thanks to the printing press, and in our century to videos, DVDs, and the Internet, we can access God's Word at any time. This Word teaches us about Jesus and His love for us. Like a mirror, the Law shows us our sins and our need for a Savior. The Law also outlines for us how we are to love and serve our Lord as His repentant children. We need not wait for Jesus to appear in our living room and begin a sermon, lecture, or discussion. Rather, His Word is constantly available to us, and His Holy Spirit is always present to enlighten us.

Through prayer and Bible study, through hearing and listening to God's Word, we eagerly follow Mary's example. She opened the door for us. Now each of God's daughters can learn, grow, be built up in love, and prepare to follow Christ's example of showing compassion to the poor, care for the suffering, and hope to the desolate.

As we grow, we thank God for the Bibles we study and for the church in which we worship Him. We thank Him, too, for the Christian organizations that provide further learning opportunities. We thank God for Christ who set a new standard of treatment for women, for Christ who wants women to learn, for Christ who offers so many opportunities for women to respond to His love and mercy by using their God-given gifts in His service. We especially thank God for sending His Son, Christ Jesus, who comes to us in His word of forgiveness as we kneel at His Table.

We also thank God for Martha and for the faith-filled response that shone through her so beautifully on the occasion of her brother's death (John 11:1–44). When Lazarus became ill, the sisters sent a messenger to Jesus to tell Him, "the one You love is sick" (v. 3 NIV). It seems likely that Jesus often stayed with the Bethany siblings. Certainly they became close friends over the years. Thus, the sisters would have been well aware of the Lord's healing power and of His miracles. Certainly they must have expected that Jesus would quickly come to His friend's side as he lay dying.

Imagine, then, Martha and Mary's shock and disappointment when Jesus delayed. Even then, His disciples objected to His return to Judea, cautioning Him that enemies near Bethany wanted to stone Him (v. 8).

The ensuing conversation is interesting. Jesus told the disciples that Lazarus had "fallen asleep," and He was going to wake him up. Why wake him? the disciples wondered. Sleep helps people get well! Finally Jesus explained in plain words what He meant: Lazarus was dead. He then went on to outline what would occur in Bethany and promised that it would enable the disciples to believe in Him even more firmly. Expecting death for Jesus, Thomas resolutely recruited the other disciples for the trip south: "Let us also go, that we may die with Him" (v. 16).

By the time they arrived, the body of Lazarus had been in the tomb for four days.[42] Many friends had gathered to comfort Martha and Mary. Ignoring her duties as hostess this time, Martha left her guests when she heard that Jesus was approaching and went out to meet Him. What a display of faith we then see. Martha obviously had spent time listening at Jesus' feet too! She regrets Jesus' absence, but she does not criticize Him for not coming sooner:

Martha said to Jesus, "Lord, if You had been here, my brother would not have died. But even now I know that whatever You ask from God, God will give You."

Jesus said to her, "Your brother will rise again."

Martha said to Him, "I know that he will rise again in the resurrection on the last day." [Most Jewish people of that day understood this.]

Jesus said to her, "I am the resurrection and the life. Whoever believes in Me, though he die, yet shall he live, and everyone who lives and believes in Me shall never die. Do you believe this?"

She said to Him, "Yes, Lord; I believe that You are the Christ, the Son of God, who is coming into the world." John 11:21–27

This beautiful statement of faith has comforted countless believers down through the centuries, and it continues to comfort us today too! Martha, like Peter (Matthew 16:16), understood and believed in Jesus as her promised Messiah.

Then Jesus asked about Mary. She was inside with the mourners. Jewish scholars tell us that for a week after the death of a close relative, mourners would have stayed in or near one's house. Visitors would have come by to express their sympathy and offer condolences. Called *shivah* (for "seven" days), this custom continues among many in Judaism still today. First-century mourners moved from this seven-day period of deep grieving into successive steps of normalization. They abstained from personal adornment for the next three weeks and from ordinary, daily pleasures for the next year.[43]

When Martha told Mary that Jesus had come and was asking for her, Mary went out immediately to greet Him. The guests followed, thinking she was going to the tomb to mourn. Their duty was to support her. Approaching Jesus, Mary fell at His feet, weeping. Jesus was "deeply moved in His spirit and greatly troubled" (John 11:33). Then comes that Bible verse, the one students love when they haven't done their memorization and are required to answer roll call with a Bible verse: "Jesus wept" (v. 35). It's the shortest verse in the Bible, yet it teaches us so much about the heart of Jesus. He truly cared about His friends' grief and responded to it with compassion. He is troubled and saddened by the human sorrows we experience.

At Jesus' request, the entire group proceeded to the tomb. His next words must have shocked everyone. He asked to have the stone removed from the entrance! Martha, ever the practical one, said out loud what everyone was thinking: By now, the odor would be unbearable; Lazarus' body had lain decomposing for four days. No one would doubt that Lazarus was dead! No one would argue that he had been in a coma or deeply asleep! Jesus answered Martha's objection: "Did I not tell you that if you believed you would see the glory of God?" (v. 40). That response expanded on His earlier statement to the disciples. For their benefit—and for ours—Jesus would demonstrate His power as the Son of God, "so that you may believe." They were about to witness a resurrection miracle!

"Lazarus, come out!" Jesus called, and Lazarus did come out, still wrapped in grave clothes! He was alive! Our all-powerful God had restored him to life. Here was undeniable proof of Jesus' power over death and the grave, the same power evident as He created the universe (Colossians 1:16). All things were and are under His power (John 13:3).

What confidence this gives us when we come to Him

in prayer. What assurance in the face of life's trials and in the face of death itself! What joy Christ offers everyone who belongs to Him through faith: "Whoever hears My word and believes Him who sent Me has eternal life" (John 5:24) and "Do you not know that all of us who have been baptized into Christ Jesus were baptized into His death?" (Romans 6:3).

Jesus Anointed for His Burial

Scripture gives us one final glimpse into the home of Martha, Mary, and Lazarus (John 12:1–9). Six days before Jesus celebrated His last Passover on earth, He stopped at Bethany on His way to the festival in Jerusalem. Martha, Mary, and Lazarus used the occasion to host a dinner in His honor. This time Scripture says only that "Martha served." It mentions nothing about her enlisting Mary.

But once again, Mary did something unorthodox. She poured a pint of pure nard on Jesus' feet as He reclined at the table. Then she wiped His feet with her hair. Nard was an expensive, musky perfume made from the roots of spikenard. This time, it was Judas Iscariot who objected: "Why was this ointment not sold for three hundred denarii and given to the poor?" (John 12:5). John explains that Judas did not really care about the poor; rather, he was a thief and, as the keeper of the disciples' treasury, he used to help himself from it (v. 6).

Again, Jesus defended Mary, this time quite strongly:

> Jesus said, "Leave her alone, so that she may keep it for the day of My burial. For the poor you always have with you, but you do not always have Me." John 12:7–8

The information in John's Gospel answers some of our

previous questions. We learn, for example, that the Bethany home was large enough to have space for reclining around tables. Also, because Mary could afford nard, those who have assumed this to be a wealthy household are probably right.

Through the actions of Martha and Mary, we also learn important truths for our own lives today.

First, Martha was an organizer, and isn't that what many of us strive to be? There's nothing wrong with good organization. Scripture tells us that everything should "be done decently and in order" (1 Corinthians 14:40). The problem comes when we grow too busy to maintain our relationship with our Lord, when our chores leave us no time for prayer or Bible study. I always marvel at Martin Luther's statement that the more he had to do, the more time he had to spend in prayer. All too often, I find myself saying, "Lord, I have a really busy day today, so please be with me. In Jesus' name, thanks! Amen." That ends my prayer time for the day, except perhaps for the "popcorn prayers" I send up to heaven in search of God's guidance throughout the day.

It seems Martha wanted everything to be perfect, down to the last detail. She undoubtedly took pride in her reputation as a homemaker and hostess. Many of us are perfectionists too, and this may cause us to get our priorities mixed up. We make daily and weekly "to do" lists and find enormous satisfaction in crossing off item after item. We may even include daily Bible study or personal devotions on the list, unaware that this potentially transforms them into a duty rather than a delight, rather than the joy of soaking up our Lord's love as we spend peaceful, quiet time with Him. Perhaps we feel a great sense of accomplishment when each day's list is completed, but by that time, we're too tired for more than a perfunctory bedtime prayer, and perhaps we even doze off before we can say "Amen." Why not take a look right now at your schedule? Does it include a date with your Lord? Imagine the joy of reading His Word and hearing Him say to you, day by day, "I am with you this day and always. I love you. I'm listening. Let's talk."

Second, Martha was comfortable sharing her concerns with Jesus. She was "distracted" (ESV), "cumbered" (KJV), until she took her problem directly to her Lord, her friend (Luke 10:40). How often we stew and complain to others before talking with the Lord or seeking the comfort of His Word. Jesus' response to Martha was caring, but firm. It reoriented Martha's priorities and reaffirmed Mary's—and it taught us something about our Savior's main concerns. Each verse, narrative, and word of Scripture serves a purpose. Each text has something to teach, some comfort to give, some wisdom to impart. From Martha and Mary, we learn about proper priorities.

But do we put that lesson into practice regularly? Do we appreciate the fact that the Son of God wants us to learn, to study His Word, to grow spiritually? What a blessing that He recognizes and affirms our ability to read, appreciate, and meditate on the message He shares with us in the Scriptures. May we always use and treasure this privilege! Even today, in many cultures around the world, women are devalued and their dignity denied. Praise God that Jesus never sanctioned such treatment and that, instead, He encouraged just the opposite.

Knowing that our Lord created us and cares for us, knowing that He understands our concerns and encourages us to share them with Him, knowing His faithful forgiveness for our sins of distraction and rebellion, we kneel with Mary at Jesus' feet. We confess our failures. We run in joy to kneel at the Communion rail where we receive our Savior's pardon and peace.

Third, Mary dared to be different. Instead of polishing the punch bowl, so to speak, she listened and learned from her guest, earning Jesus' commendation. When Martha heard Jesus was coming, she went to meet Him, but Mary "stayed at home" (John 11:20), weeping in the house amidst the noisy, wailing mourners. At the dinner honoring Jesus, Mary anointed His feet with exquisite perfume, which Jesus recognized as pointing to His burial. By showing her love in this way, she honored the Lord and initiated the bodily preparations for His death. The disciples still didn't understand that Jesus would soon die. Did Mary?

True, her actions were out of the ordinary, unusual, unexpected. What about us today? Do we dare to be different? Do we regularly repent of our sins, bask in Christ's forgiveness, and rely on Him for strength to change our behaviors? Do we recognize Christ as the bread of life in Holy Communion and look forward with longing to receiving Him? Do we count on the presence of His Spirit to invigorate our witness and enable us to serve the poor, the distressed, the sick as He did? Are we willing to touch, assist, and be seen with those who are elderly, indigent, handicapped, different—those whom Matthew 25:40 calls "the least of these"? Do we daily give thanks for the opportunities Christ offers and the loving heart He shows to all people?

None of us can perfectly keep God's Law. We are distracted by our daily lives, by our responsibilities and obligations, by our own sinful, selfish nature. Certainly we want to care for our families and serve those around us who need our care. Of course, it is not appropriate to ignore or neglect our duties.

Even so, Jesus invites us to take time to be passive, to receive Him. As we read His Word, as we meditate on His promises, He fills us with His Spirit and showers us with

His grace. When we let go of our inner compulsive busyness, the Gospel can sink in. Responding to His gifts, we kneel at His Table and receive the holy gifts He, in love, holds out to us!

The Heart of Jesus as Shown in the Lives of Mary and Martha

Women are important to Christ as believers, co-workers, and, above all, as learners. He wants us to grow in His love, in His peace, and in our worship lives. Today, as He has always done, He comes to us personally to gift us with His grace and mercy.

Chapter NINE

The Crippled Woman

Humble Worshiper, Thankful Beneficiary
Luke 13:10–17

Now [Jesus] was teaching in one of the synagogues on the Sabbath. And there was a woman who had had a disabling spirit for eighteen years. She was bent over and could not fully straighten herself. When Jesus saw her, He called her over and said to her, "Woman, you are freed from your disability." Luke 13:10–12

[Jesus said,] "Does not each of you on the Sabbath untie his ox or his donkey from the manger and lead it away to water it? And ought not this woman, a daughter of Abraham whom Satan bound for eighteen years, be loosed from this bond on the Sabbath day?" As He said these things, all His adversaries were put to shame, and all the people rejoiced at all the glorious things that were done by Him. Luke 13:15b–17

153

Friends of mine who gave birth to a developmentally disabled daughter became convinced God was punishing them for some sin. They didn't know what sin, but they had no doubt that their baby's disability was a punishment from God. They took good care of her, but initially they did little to learn about her condition or about how they might help her advance. They didn't realize that developmentally disabled people can learn, progress, and develop—more slowly and in different ways, to be sure, but they can indeed progress. These parents simply accepted their plight.

That attitude is nothing new; it's been around for centuries. Well before the time of Christ, the view of God as angry and vindictive pervaded many cultures. As one result of this, people with disabilities often have been relegated to the margins of society.

Because this view was common in first-century Israel as well, the woman described in Luke 13 had likely accepted her plight in resignation and humility also. Although she faithfully made her way to worship, she did not come forward of her own volition to seek healing from Jesus. She did not push her way to the front of the synagogue, hoping for help. Instead, Jesus took the initiative. He called her forward. Then, with just a few words and the touch of His hands, He healed her.

Imagine her joy and surprise! After eighteen years—"long years," as the NIV puts it—she could now stand tall and walk easily. Her deformity and her pain were gone! After eighteen years of having to walk slowly and carefully, perhaps hobbling with a cane, she now could move freely and without discomfort. After eighteen years, she could look people in the eye. After eighteen years of depending on others, of being unable to do all that she desired in her home, of having to ask for help, she was finally liberated from her infirmity. After eighteen years of bondage to Satan, she was free.

Most likely she had kept to one side of the footpaths and roadways she traversed, staying out of people's way as much as possible, not wanting to inconvenience them or slow them down. Some may have passed by without a word or even a glance. Others may have looked at her with pity or even with a sneer that suggested, "Why doesn't she just stay at home, out of sight?" Perhaps, like Job's "comforters," well-meaning friends had even suggested she repent of the sin that had brought on the condition.[44]

But now, now on this Sabbath Day, everyone scrutinized her with wonder and curiosity. It was hard to believe that Jesus, so busy and always surrounded by so many people, had even noticed her in the crowd. It was even harder to believe He had called her forward. She would never have dared to approach Him! How amazed she must have been to think that this famous teacher had taken notice of her, a poor, crippled woman. How amazed she must have been when He immediately stopped what He was doing and healed her, especially on this sacred day.

Oh, how she must have thanked Him! How fervently she must have praised God!

But suddenly, the synagogue ruler cut her expressions of gratitude short. Indignant, he began to express the outrage of many in attendance. Didn't Jesus understand the commandment about keeping the Sabbath Day holy? God's people must not work on that day! They could work all they wanted for six days, but the seventh day was the Lord's Day.

Remember the Sabbath Day!

Still today, Orthodox Jews follow the Old Testament laws regarding rest on the Lord's Day. Just as God Himself rested on the seventh day of creation, so observant Jews consider Saturday a holy day of sacred assembly on which no work is to be done.[45] Since Old Testament times, the Sabbath has begun at sundown Friday evening and continued until sundown Saturday evening.

To make sure everyone understood what that meant, the Old Testament rabbis developed numerous explanatory rules. These prohibited the thirty-nine types of work common during the time the temple was being built and included tasks like carrying or transporting, burning, extinguishing, finishing, writing, erasing, cooking (baking), washing, sewing, tearing, knotting, untying, shaping, plowing, planting, repairing, harvesting (including binding sheaves), threshing, winnowing, selecting, sifting, grinding, kneading, combing, spinning, dyeing, chain-stitching, warping, weaving, unraveling, building (hitting anything with a hammer), demolishing, trapping, shearing (including cutting hair or fingernails), slaughtering, skinning, tanning, smoothing or polishing, and marking (drawing lines).[46]

These prohibitions became more elaborate as time went on. For example, the law against burning was later interpreted to include lighting a fire, whether directly or indirectly. This evolved later still into a prohibition against using an electrical switch. Therefore, observant Orthodox Jews today refrain from striking a match, turning on a light, igniting a stove burner, pushing an elevator button, or changing a thermostat to start a furnace on the Sabbath. Since they do want candles burning for the Sabbath meal, women are careful to light their candles eighteen minutes before sunset. The light in the refrigerator is turned off before sunset so it will not come on when someone in the household opens the refrigerator door. Orthodox Jews try to live within walking distance of their synagogue because starting a car's engine involves igniting fuel and moving or carrying objects.

Our Lord intended the Sabbath Day as a blessing, a gift He wanted to give His people. In today's culture, a culture in which many people expect to work a five-day week, we may not appreciate the Sabbath as a gift. Not so in ancient times! Then, only rulers and the very wealthy could afford to take leisure time. Societies around Israel viewed the Jews as lazy because they rested every seventh day.[47] The legalism that grew up around the Sabbath laws given on Mount Sinai eventually extracted much of the joy God intended when He gave His people this good gift.

We see evidence of legalism's hardened crust in the ultra-orthodox synagogue ruler of Luke 13. He just couldn't believe his eyes—such a respected rabbi as Jesus, healing on a day of rest! "There are six days in which work ought to be done," he said. "Come on those days and be healed, and not on the Sabbath day" (Luke 13:14).

We might say that the synagogue ruler was disabled too—by his own self-righteousness. He was bound as tightly by his close-mindedness as the woman had been by her physical ailment. Jesus minced no words in pointing this out. "You hypocrites!" He exclaimed, looking around at the smug, critical expressions. Then He asked, "Don't each of you on the Sabbath untie your ox or donkey from the stall and lead it out to give it water?" Of course they did. They couldn't deny it.

"And," He asked, "ought not this woman, a daughter of Abraham whom Satan bound for eighteen years, be loosed from this bond on the Sabbath day?" His question humiliated His opponents. It was their turn to hide their heads in shame, while the woman who had been healed stood erect, her head held high. This turn of events delighted the nonlegalists in the room, and Jesus' reputation grew.

This passage includes several interesting aspects. First, consider the question of where disabilities originate. Jesus plainly states that "Satan bound her." This healing miracle again demonstrates Christ's power over Satan.

Second, Jesus emphasizes that when someone has a problem and others can help, they are obligated to do so immediately—regardless of the letter of the Mosaic Law. In this way, He asserts His authority as the Lawgiver. He is, as He claimed to be, "lord of the Sabbath" (Luke 6:5).

Third, Jesus calls the woman He healed a "daughter of Abraham." In Old Testament times, lineage was normally traced through sons, so we often see the words "son of Abraham" or "son of Isaac," but this is the only instance in all of Scripture where a woman is identified as a "daughter of Abraham." In using this description, Jesus clearly defines her value in the eyes of God Himself. Although others may have viewed her as worthless because of her disability, He sees her as a person of worth and dignity.

As Scripture clearly indicates, our Lord sees us in this same way. We often struggle with this. It's easy to denigrate ourselves as we think about our shortcomings and, especially, our sins. Probably all of us have from time to time wished we could change some minor physical imperfection—big feet, a crooked nose, weak eyes that make glasses necessary. Some of us, of course, bear much more serious burdens—the inability to see, hear, speak, move or think clearly and logically. Still, many have overcome obstacles like these and have lived not merely ordinary, but rather, extraordinary lives, lives that have greatly benefited society and the Church.

Consider a few examples of individuals of accomplishment, people who have contributed substantially to the quality of life here on earth despite pronounced mental and physical challenges. You likely know the stories of many women who belong on a list like that. My own favorite examples include Fanny Crosby (1820–1915), the prolific hymnwriter who was blind; Helen Keller (1880–1968), the deaf-blind author whose works have been published in many languages; and Joni Eareckson Tada (1950-), the quadriplegic disability advocate whose work has touched lives for Christ around the world.

Fanny Crosby

Frances Jane (Fanny) Crosby[48] developed an eye infection when she was less than two months old. She became blind when an inept doctor prescribed hot mustard poultices.

One could assume Crosby would have prayed often for the return of her eyesight. Not so! While still a child, Fanny resolved never to be unhappy about her situation. She said she felt no resentment toward the "doctor," believing her condition was part of God's purpose for her life. She told people that the blessing of being blind was that the first face she would see would be that of her Lord in heaven. She also believed that she might not have written all the hymns she had if she had been distracted by seeing all the beautiful and interesting things in her surroundings.

Widowed just a year after Fanny was born, Crosby's mother had to work to provide for the family. This meant that Crosby's grandmother often cared for her. Her grandmother regularly read the Bible to Crosby, and soon she had memorized many Scripture verses. Sometimes, she learned four or five chapters a week! As you might imagine, this provided a meaningful foundation when she began writing hymns.

Crosby longed for a formal education. She was overjoyed when, nearing age 15, she was able to enter the New York Institution for the Blind. Fanny stayed there for 23 years, twelve as a student and eleven on the faculty. Exposed to history, philosophy, and good literature at the school, she also learned to play the organ, guitar, and piano. As a child, she had begun writing poetry. While at the Institution, she published two books of poems; a third followed soon after she left.

When the Institution sought a federal grant to support its work, Crosby, then age 23, was among the students taken to Washington, D.C., to testify before Congress. She gave no speech, but simply recited some of her poems. Her poetry brought tears to the eyes of the congressmen. This led to friendships with a number of presidents, including Martin Van Buren, William Henry Harrison, John Tyler, James Polk, and Grover Cleveland. Cleveland actually served for a period as secretary of the Institution for the Blind.

In 1858, Fanny left the Institution and married Alexander Van Alstyne, a fellow pupil who also had become a teacher at the facility. He was an excellent organist and later composed the music for some of her hymns. After their marriage, a pastor introduced Fanny to William Bradbury, a well-known composer. He encouraged her to switch from poetry to hymns, and in 1863, she completed her first, "There's a Cry from Macedonia." From then until her death at age 95, Crosby continued to write hymns, sometimes several in a single day. Some estimate she wrote as many as nine thousand, but it is difficult to be sure, because she also wrote under about two hundred pseudonyms!

Crosby's hymns gained popularity as they were sung in the evangelistic campaigns of Dwight Moody and later by George Beverly Shea in Billy Graham crusades. Among the most famous are "Blessed Assurance"; "To God Be the Glory"; "Pass Me Not, O Gentle Savior"; "Christ, the Lord,

Is Risen Today"; "Safe in the Arms of Jesus"; "Rescue the Perishing"; and "He Hideth My Soul."

Helen Keller

Diagnosed with "brain fever" at the age of 19 months, Helen Keller became not only blind but also deaf. She has been called "the most famous handicapped person in the world." Keller succeeded against overwhelming odds, becoming a persistent and sensitive spokesperson for the good of others.[49]

Keller's story, of course, has been told and retold in the play and movie *The Miracle Worker*. From Keller's viewpoint, her life began at age 7, when Anne Sullivan, who was partially blind herself, arrived at Helen's home to become her teacher. Anne started by spelling words into Helen's hand. It meant nothing, however, until Anne put Helen's hand into water gushing from an outdoor pump and spelled "w-a-t-e-r" into her hand. By evening that same day, Helen knew and had connected thirty words with their meanings!

By age 10, Keller was learning to speak. In 1900, she entered Radcliffe College, graduating *summa cum laude* in 1904. Although that concluded her formal schooling, she received several honorary doctorates for her work as a writer of books, magazine articles, and newspaper stories dealing with such varied subjects as blindness, deafness, socialism, social issues, and women's rights.[50] She used both Braille and conventional typewriters.

Keller's works have been translated into more than fifty languages, and she has been honored for her accomplishments by many countries around the world, including Brazil, Japan, Lebanon, and the Philippines. Her birthplace in Tuscumbia, Alabama, is now a national shrine.

During her lifetime, Keller visited more than thirty-five countries on five continents. Always seeking ways to help those "less fortunate than myself," Helen served on numerous boards and did extensive fund-raising for the American Foundation for the Blind (AFB).[51] In her later years, she spent much time reading. The Bible was one of her favorite books.

Joni Eareckson Tada

When you have lived a typical life for seventeen years and suddenly find yourself unable to move your arms or legs, life gets tough. That's what happened to Joni Eareckson when she took a reckless dive into shallow water. The result: crushed vertebrae and a severed spinal cord. The diagnosis: complete paralysis from the shoulders down. She would be a quadriplegic for the rest of her life.

Understandably, Joni wanted to die, and she begged friends to help her commit suicide. They refused. Today, she is most grateful, so grateful that she campaigns against euthanasia and assisted suicide.

The Lord has used her to help others in many other ways as well. Joni realizes this would not have happened without her injury. She describes herself as a wayward lamb before her accident, living a "normal," typically self-focused teenage lifestyle. Then came the day of her accident, and everything changed.

While in rehab, Joni learned to write by holding a pencil in her mouth. Soon after, she began to draw and paint using the same method. Her talent soon brought her much acclaim and invitations to appear on national TV shows. In 1979, she founded Joni and Friends (JAF) to facilitate and encourage Christian ministry in the disability community around the world. This led to the construction of the Joni and Friends International Disability Center in 2006. It houses a new communications center as well as a training facility for JAF international partnerships. It also includes the Christian Institute on Disability, whose goal is to influence public thinking on disability-related issues such as euthanasia and stem-cell research.

Although Joni's major interest is motivating churches to reach out and include people with disabilities, her influence extends far beyond the Christian community. In addition to serving on governmental disability councils, she was appointed in 2005 to the Disability Advisory Committee of the U.S. State Department. In this capacity, she has advised Dr. Condoleezza Rice on policy and programs that affect disabled persons in the State Department and around the world.[52]

Her efforts have touched the lives of millions. More than a thousand radio stations air her daily five-minute radio program. JAF sponsors fifteen annual family retreats nationwide, serving more than eight hundred special-needs families. Her Wheels for the World program has collected more than thirty thousand wheelchairs nationwide. They are refurbished by inmates in seventeen correctional facilities across the United States and then shipped to developing nations, where they are given free of charge to needy disabled children and adults. Whenever possible, the group of Christians assisting with the distribution includes at least one therapist who fits each chair to its new owner.

A popular TV guest and conference speaker both in the United States and overseas, Joni has authored more than thirty-five books on many disability-related topics, including suffering, death, heaven, healing, physician-assisted suicide, and other right-to-life issues. Her story has been told in numerous biographies; in her personal memoir, *The God I Love*; and in the movie *Joni*. Her most recent venture involves creating and hosting a new television program,

Joni and Friends, which offers a refreshingly honest approach to people's toughest questions about the goodness
of God in a world shattered by pain and suffering.

Needless to say, all this has not gone unnoticed by
educational institutions and Christian associations. Joni
has received four honorary doctorates and many special
awards. Her husband, Ken Tada, a retired high-school
teacher, works alongside her in all these endeavors. They
were married in 1982.

The Church's Challenge

As the lives of Fanny Crosby, Helen Keller, and Joni
Eareckson Tada illustrate, people with disabilities have
great value. Countless thousands who never achieve fame
like that of Crosby, Keller, and Tada nevertheless serve
faithfully in many roles, living out many life vocations.
Thanks to special-education programs, supportive employers, wheelchair-accessible buildings and transportation,
curb-cuts, prostheses, talking computers, and other adap-
tive technology, these people live productive lives. Many
have even started their own outreach ministries, bringing
Christian encouragement to others.

The challenge to the Church is that of following our
Lord's example of outreach to those often undervalued
and ignored by society. When the apostle Paul described
the Church in terms of a human body, he reminded us that
"the parts of the body that seem to be weaker are indispensable" (1 Corinthians 12:33). As he explained, "The eye
cannot say to the hand, 'I have no need of you,' nor again
the head to the feet, 'I have no need of you'" (v. 21). Nevertheless, Christian congregations have often communicated
just that to people with disabilities, whether physical, intel-
lectual, or emotional.

With at least five hundred million disabled persons in the world and an estimated forty-nine million of them in the United States, the challenge is huge. Add the families and relatives of these disabled individuals, and one finds that at least fifty percent of the world's people are touched in one way or another by this challenge.

So how can the Church help meet their needs? By sharing Christ's love. By caring. By advocating. By including people with disabilities in our planning, policies, and practice.

For centuries, little of this was done anywhere in the world, especially in relation to developmental disabilities, then identified as "mental retardation." However, there were rare exceptions.

In the fourth century, St. Nicholas of Myra, known today as Santa Claus, served as a patron and guardian of young children. He was recognized especially for the tender care he gave to many individuals then called "idiots" and "imbeciles."

As French doctors began learning more about mental disabilities in the eighteenth century, they concluded that mental retardation is not mental illness. This led to the establishment of the first secular school for people with retardation in Paris in 1839.

A few decades later, German Christians began developing colonies for people with mental retardation. Most notable was Bethel at Bielefeld in Ravensberger province. Progress began when a young pastor, Frederick von Bodelschwingh, was assigned to the small, struggling home. As this colony of mercy grew, it spawned fifty-nine homes for people with epilepsy and other disabilities, as well as for the "weary poor and the retired rich," criminals, drunkards, and orphans—all who were homeless.

Despite this progress, prejudice against people with disabilities continued. On the other side of the ocean, a similar situation prevailed. When the American colonies were established, people with disabilities were refused admission; authorities feared they would require financial support. In Puritan New England, many individuals with physical and mental disabilities were burned at the stake or stoned to death during witch-hunts. Segregation of people with mental disabilities was officially sanctioned by state legislatures, who passed laws declaring them unfit for citizenship.[53]

In 1773, the first U.S. hospital for disabled people was founded in Williamsburg, Virginia. More like a prison than a hospital, it housed criminals, vagrants, poor people, those with mental illness, and those with mental retardation. Regardless of condition, everyone lived together.

Eventually hospitals similar to this one were built across the country, but soon separate institutions were established for "mental defectives," many with a thousand to fifteen hundred residents. By the 1900s, people had begun to view mental retardation as hereditary; they also linked it with criminal behavior. The so-called "Eugenics Movement" seemed to give scientific sanction for the involuntary sterilization of disabled persons, theoretically to prevent the country from being overrun by feebleminded criminals! Indiana passed a law mandating compulsory sterilization of "degenerates" in 1907. In Europe, there were calls for euthanasia of "defectives." When Hitler came into power, people with mental retardation and mental illness became the first guinea pigs for Nazi Germany's medical experiments and mass executions.

Eventually, true scientific research and wiser heads began to prevail. When the stock market crashed in 1929, some individuals from formerly wealthy families succumbed to depression and other mental illnesses. It became increasingly obvious that the role of environment in creating social problems was at least as great as the role of heredity and that, in any case, segregation and murder were not viable treatment options.

Christians Get Involved

Against this sad history, where was the Church? Sad to say, mostly silent until the early 1900s, when the Lutheran Church—Missouri Synod and several other denominations began opening institutions to serve people with developmental disabilities. There, residents received loving care, opportunities to learn viable work skills, and, most important, instruction in the Christian faith. Often the residents' devout trust in Jesus set an example for those who served them.

In time, these large residential facilities were depopulated and the residents moved into less restrictive settings—group homes and community apartments. That change challenged many more individual congregations to engage in inclusive, Christlike ministry.

Similar developments can be traced in the field of deaf and blind services. There, too, Christians picked up the ball by

- *calling chaplains to serve people in state-run facilities;*

- *founding service organizations like Lutheran Braille Workers; and*

- *adding staff to national church body offices to develop resources and train and encourage congregations in disability outreach.*

Such outreach is becoming even more important with the realization that as people live longer, most of us at some time in life will experience disability. We may one day lose our hearing, our eyesight, or our facility in getting around. We may need special glasses, hearing aids, canes, walkers, or wheelchairs.

Does your congregation provide large-print bulletins, hymnals, and Bibles? If your church projects hymns and announcements on screens, do you make printed versions available for those who cannot see the screen clearly? How does your congregation accommodate the needs of those who need help hearing the sermon or accessing the various levels of your building? Have you provided a few shorter pews so people in wheelchairs can sit beside relatives and friends rather than parking illegally in the aisle, conspicuously in the front, or invisibly in the back where their line of vision is obstructed? None of these accommodations is relatively expensive. And they speak much more loudly than your words about your care—and Christ's care—for every individual.

As individual disciples of our Savior, we want to demonstrate His attitude of concern and respect. That means treating people who have disabilities the same way we treat our friends. Some of the simplest approaches are also the most appreciated and helpful:

- *Be yourself while showing each disabled person the same respect you wish them to show you.*

- *Offer assistance, but don't force it upon someone.*

- *Listen well and courteously.*

- *Speak naturally, talking directly to the disabled person, not only to his or her attendant or companion.*

- *Speak at your normal rate and volume unless the person also has a hearing impairment.*

- *Offer to pray with the person when she or he indicates a special need.*

- *When you communicate with someone who has a cognitive disability, use simple sentences, make your instructions clear and concise, and do not be condescending. Speak to the person even if he or she is not verbal enough to respond.*

- *Use "people first" language. People with a disability are "people with a disability," not "the disabled."*

- *Allow persons with disabilities to do things for themselves if they want, even if it takes longer.*

These approaches don't take a lot of work, but they do require awareness and sensitivity. They clearly communicate the idea that as God's people, we value each individual, and so does Christ. People with disabilities play an indispensable role in our mission and ministry.

Whether or not we live with a disability, each person has worth and dignity. We are each created in the image of God. Of course, if we are honest, we recognize that we are all "disabled" by both original and actual sin. Only Jesus lived a perfect life. He lived that life for us, in our place. And then He died an agonizing death on the cross in full payment for all our sins. Now, God credits Christ's righteousness to our account. In Him, we have become righteous in God's sight. Now, He has entrusted us with the message of salvation, inviting and commanding us to share it with all who will hear.

This includes people with disabilities. Just as Jesus demonstrated His concern for the woman in Luke 13, so, too, we can demonstrate His compassion to the people with special needs who come across our path. Just as Jesus called the crippled woman to Himself and healed her, so, too, He calls us to share His healing hope and encouragement. What an honor.

The Heart of Jesus as Shown in the Life of the Crippled Woman

Christ has compassion on each of us, sinners all. He values every human being, including people with disabilities. Our Lord calls His Church and the individual members of His Body to continue the work He began. Because we know His mercy toward us, we can joyfully share that mercy with others.

The Persistent Widow, The Woman with the Lost Coin and The Poor Widow

Determined Seeker, Persevering Plaintiff, Generous Donor

Luke 18:1–8; 15:8–10; 21:1–4

[Jesus said,] "In a certain city there was a judge who neither feared God nor respected man. And there was a widow . . . who kept coming to him and saying, 'Give me justice against my adversary.' For a while he refused, but afterward he said to himself, '. . . because this widow keeps bothering me, I will give her justice. . . .' And the Lord said, '. . . will not God give justice to His elect . . . ?'" Luke 18:2–6

Jesus looked up and saw the rich putting their gifts into the offering box, and He saw a poor widow put in two small copper coins. And He said, "Truly, I tell you, this poor widow has put in more than all of them. For they all contributed out of their abundance, but she out of her poverty put in all she had to live on." Luke 21:1–4

What woman, having ten silver coins, if she loses one coin, does not light a lamp and sweep the house and seek diligently until she finds it? And when she has found it, she calls together her friends and neighbors, saying, "Rejoice with me, for I have found the coin that I had lost." Just so, I tell you, there is joy before the angels of God over one sinner who repents. Luke 15:8–10

"Read me a story!" "Tell me a story!"

How often mothers, grandmothers, aunts, and others hear requests like these from young children in the family! Listening to stories read aloud by a caring adult is a favorite pastime of youngsters, even in this era of digital entertainment. Children love to snuggle up in the arms of a loving relative or friend and listen to their favorite story—again and again and again.

My love of Bible stories developed because of a second-grade Sunday School teacher who rewarded us for careful attention to the lesson by reading to us from her big Bible story book at the end of each class. I've forgotten all my other Sunday School teachers, but I still remember Miss Arlene Olmstead because of that book and those stories.[54]

As Jesus taught, He often chose to tell stories with a message; we call them parables. Each emphasized a truth the Lord wanted to convey. Jesus based His parables on the culture of His day, His knowledge of human nature, and on the goals He had in mind for the learners who sat listening to His teachings, but not on specific historical occurrences. There are more than thirty parables, and perhaps as many as sixty, depending on how we define the term. Matthew, Mark, and Luke record Christ's parables, but arguably John does not include any examples of this genre—again, depending on one's definition. Most simply, parables have been described as "earthly stories with a heavenly meaning."

The term itself in the Greek of the New Testament means something "thrown alongside." In general terms, the earthly story line of the parable lies parallel to a single main spiritual truth drawn from the kingdom of God. Jesus intended His parables to help believers grow in their knowledge of God. They offered other benefits too. As believers allowed the parables to sink in, they often found themselves confronting sin in their lives; parables have a way of seeping in under and around the barriers of defensiveness human beings often raise. Listeners might reject a direct accusation with a meaning that's immediately apparent. A parable, though, often slips in and does its work before we can raise our defenses. Finally, parables are memorable! To this day, we remember the ones we learned in early childhood with little effort.

Let's look at two parables and one narrative, each describing a woman who faced a serious problem. They teach us much about our Lord, His will for us, and the compassion He showers on us.

The Persistent Widow

The Old Testament uses strong language regarding the Lord's concern for widows and His protective, passionate defense of them. For example:

You shall not mistreat any widow or fatherless

*child. If you do mistreat them, and they cry out
to Me, I will surely hear their cry, and My wrath
will burn, and I will kill you with the sword,
and your wives shall become widows and your
children fatherless. Exodus 22:22–24*

Elsewhere, God calls Himself "the protector of widows" (Psalm 68:5). He promises to sustain them (Psalm 146:9). In Isaiah 1:17, He urges all His people to "seek justice, correct oppression . . . [and] plead the widow's cause."

The persistent widow Jesus describes in Luke 18 certainly needed someone to plead her case. It's hard to imagine a judge who "neither feared God nor respected man." One wonders how such a person rose to such a high position of responsibility! Nevertheless, that was the situation this woman faced—a totally uncaring judge.

"Give me justice against my adversary," she pleaded. Her request fell on deaf ears. Jesus does not tell us anything about her adversary or about the specifics of her case. Perhaps she was losing her home. Perhaps she owed a debt, like the widow in 2 Kings 4:1–7, whose God-fearing husband had died owing money to someone. When that lender in 2 Kings came to take the widow's two boys as slaves in payment for the debt, all she had of value was a little oil. "Go to your neighbors and get all the empty jars you can find," the prophet Elisha told her when she sought his help. Then, following his instructions, she poured oil into all the jars, kettles, and containers she could find. The oil kept flowing until every vessel was full. She sold the oil, paid her debt, and used the money that was left to support herself and her sons. Quite a "pension plan"!

The widow in Luke 18 had no Elisha to help her. All she could do was continue to plead with the judge. She obviously could not afford a lawyer, so she just kept coming back to court again and again. Finally the judge decided,

"Because this widow keeps bothering me, I will see that she gets justice, so that she won't eventually wear me out with her coming!" Even then, he was concerned for himself, not her.

That's not how it is with God, Jesus emphasized. In contrast, He asked (Luke 18:7), "And will not God give justice to His elect, who cry to Him day and night? Will He delay long over them?" Obviously not! In fact, the parable's point pivots on this contrast! Reassuringly, Jesus here promises that our Lord will see that His people get justice—and quickly.

That parable reminds us of another that Jesus told emphasizing the importance of bold prayer. In Luke 11:5–13, He described a man who needed some bread because a guest had arrived late at night and he had nothing in the house to offer. Although it was midnight, the host went to a friend to ask for three loaves. The man refused. His children were already in bed, and the door was locked. If the home was small and the children were sleeping on pallets on the floor, it may have been very difficult to get to his bread supply without waking the youngsters. Nevertheless, because the host persisted, the friend gave in. The story ends with this great promise:

> Ask, and it will be given to you; seek, and you
> will find; knock, and it will be opened to you.
> For everyone who asks receives, and the one
> who seeks finds, and to the one who knocks it
> will be opened. Luke 11:9–10

God's promises to us go further still! Just as a father will not give his son a snake when he asks for a fish, or a scorpion when he wants an egg, so our Father in heaven will give us the best gift of all—the Holy Spirit (Luke 11:13). We need only ask.

The point in all these texts is God's faithful care for His people. He will satisfy all our true needs in His perfect timing. Therefore, we can "always . . . pray and not lose heart." Luke 18:1 says just that, and names it as the very reason Jesus first told the parable of the persistent widow. It's also why He told the parable of the man needing bread; that parable came right on the heels of His teaching the Lord's Prayer. "Teach us to pray," they had said. "And keep on praying," these parables add.

Some people believe that after you have prayed for something once, you need not pray about it again. "God hears the first time," they reason. That's true, but these parables tell us to keep on praying until the Lord's answer is clear. Don't give up—keep on seeking, asking, knocking. God wants us to be in regular communication with Him until the right time comes for Him to supply our need or until the reason for His delay or denial is clear.

Then, when our Savior answers, we remember to thank Him! In fact, He wants us to thank Him constantly, even in the midst of our troubles. Scripture says we are to "give thanks in all circumstances; for this is the will of God in Christ Jesus for you" (1 Thessalonians 5:18). Note that the passage says "*in* all circumstances," not "*for* all circumstances." No matter how bad things may seem, those who know and love Jesus can find something in them for which we can be thankful. Our joy comes in remembering "that for those who love God all things work together for good" (Romans 8:28).

The Woman Who Lost a Valuable Coin

Luke groups the parable of the woman and the lost coin with two others about loss—the shepherd who lost a sheep and the father who lost a son. Together, these parables give us a greater understanding of our heavenly

Father's relentless love for us, His continuous search for the lost, and His delight at our return to Him. The shepherd is a picture of Jesus, the Good Shepherd, who cares for every lamb entrusted to His care. The father shows us how God the Father rejoices—ecstatically!—at the return of His wayward children, and the woman demonstrates how continuously the Holy Spirit works until the lost are found.

The woman in the parable had lost a valuable coin. Perhaps her husband had entrusted it to her. It likely represented about a day's wages. Undoubtedly, the couple was poor and needed every cent he earned. More likely, the money was one-tenth of her dowry. According to the custom of the day, a bride brought dowry money into the marriage; if the relationship later dissolved,[55] this money remained technically hers. Women often sewed their dowry money into their headdress for safekeeping.[56] If some stitches let loose over time, one of the coins could easily drop to the floor.

Floors in those days were usually packed dirt or clay and often were covered with uneven stones with cracks between them. Coins and other small objects often fell and got lost in these cracks. Moreover, the houses had no picture windows to admit the light that would have made it easy to spot a lost object. The woman in Jesus' story lit a candle or a small lamp, but it was little help. Hers would have been a tiny, hand-held oil lamp that gave only flickering light. It was no easy job to find that missing coin. She anxiously swept and swept, hoping to hear it rattle or perhaps sparkle just a bit in the faint glimmer of her light.

Then, at last—success! How relieved she was! In fact, in her joy, she hurried to tell her friends and the other women in the neighborhood. "Rejoice with me, for I have found the coin that I had lost," she told them.

Jesus then draws attention to His story's point: "In the

same way, I tell you, there is rejoicing in the presence of the angels of God over one sinner who repents." Our loving Lord wants everyone to be saved. He does not want anyone to perish (2 Peter 3:9). Each individual matters to Him. That's why He tells these parables about losing, seeking, finding, and rejoicing. That's why He sent the Holy Spirit as our Counselor and Comforter to convict us of our sin, lead us to repentance, testify to Christ, and transform us into His likeness (John 14:26; 15:26; 16:7–8; 2 Corinthians 3:18). That's why He wants us to share His Good News and seek the lost. We often mourn for unbelievers, but this parable teaches us that we must do more than mourn. We must seek them out. We must search diligently for them as the woman did for her coin.

Jesus told this parable and its two companion stories because the Pharisees and the teachers of the law were criticizing Him for associating with sinners who were the outcasts of their day. All three stories stress the importance of reaching out to those who are lost.

What does that mean for us—for you and me? For many Christians, it has meant trip after trip to Louisiana and Mississippi to assist the homeless with rebuilding after Hurricane Katrina. For others, it has meant short- or long-term mission trips, helping with a local VBS, and other efforts to share the Gospel with those who do not know Jesus—both at home and in foreign countries. For still others, it may mean staffing food pantries, providing clothing for the poor, volunteering in thrift stories run by charities, filling sand bags, or serving meals to the hungry.

In short, these parables and Christ's command to "make disciples of all nations" (Matthew 28:19) require more than praying, although that's important too. The parables mandate a willingness to share our time, talents, and treasures wherever and whenever the Lord calls us to do that—both inside and outside the walls of our churches.

All that we do, we do in response to Christ's love for us. Jesus acted on our behalf in love that went beyond anything the world had ever seen or will see again. He left His heavenly home to live the perfect life we could never live and then to offer Himself on the altar of the cross as the perfect sacrifice for our sins. When He returned to heaven, He did not leave us to fend for ourselves; He sent His Holy Spirit to seek us out, teach us, and encourage us in our response to His love. And so, as Jesus indicated in His explanation of the parable, the rejoicing goes on and on, today and forever in heaven, as the lost are found and brought back into His fold!

The Poor Widow

Most of us find it difficult to share our "treasure." I know I have. Having lived through the Great Depression, I tend to hoard things. I keep clothes that are out of style, even some that no longer fit—they might come back in style again, and someday I hope to lose some weight. I save buttons (always helpful if I lose one), pictures and souvenirs (when I'm old and can't get out, they'll be fun to look at), books (someday I hope to read them all), hats (one came in handy when I went to a fiftieth-anniversary dinner for which we were supposed to dress as they did fifty years ago), and my children's toys (my grandchildren might like them). The list could go on and on.

In the back of my mind, I think about the possibility that I might become poor again. When I was a child, my family was so poor that I had just two pairs of socks and one pair of shoes. They had to last for a year.

We lived in South Dakota during the Dust Bowl years. The winds were so strong that they blew dust through the floorboards and caused our linoleum kitchen rug to rise like a flying carpet. Fine dust settled throughout the house, and getting rid of it all took cleaning after cleaning.

That wasn't the only problem. Grasshoppers ate our crops and forced my dad to put the few household items we owned into a truck and move us to Wisconsin. There we lived with relatives until he was able to get a temporary job.

When that ended, my dad worked for the WPA for months, improving city streets. During that time, my mother needed surgery for a tumor on her arm. We could not afford it, but because Dad was a WPA employee, the government paid for it. Soon she was healed, and my dad obtained a permanent job that enabled us to live comfortably in a series of one- and two-room apartments until my parents had saved enough to buy a four-room house. Our own home at last—we thought we were in heaven!

One wonders about the challenges faced by the widow Jesus saw in the temple. She had only two copper coins, and she put both of them into the temple treasury. Each was worth about 1/128 of a denarius, and a denarius was one day's pay for a common laborer. If we compare her with someone earning $10 an hour today, her offering would have equaled about $1.25.

What were her options after she left the temple? Live off the charity of her neighbors or a relative? Depend on the temple to supply her needs? Beg? Die? We don't know, but we can consider her trust and generosity with amazement!

Jesus contrasted her gift with that of the rich people who came to put much greater amounts of money into the temple receptacles. They give out of their wealth, Jesus notes, "but she out of her poverty put in all she had to live on" (Luke 21:4).

Could you do that? I don't think I could, unless I expected to go right home and die. The widow did not give to gain attention, like some of the wealthy people who conspicuously placed their gifts in one of the temple's trumpet-shaped collection vessels and then returned home to continue living in luxury. Although the widow did nothing to call attention to herself, Jesus saw her. He noticed her, just as He noticed the crippled woman at the back of the synagogue.

In compassion, Jesus regularly noticed the needy, even when there were other demands on Him. The incident with the widow took place during Holy Week, the week of our Lord's Passion and death. From the moment of His triumphal entry into Jerusalem on Palm Sunday, He had been dealing with nearly nonstop confrontation. First, the Pharisees criticized the crowds who praised Him in the words of the psalmist: "Blessed is the King who comes in the name of the Lord!" (Luke 19:38). Grumbling, the Pharisees urged Christ to rebuke them, to stop their shouts and songs of praise. They were disturbing the peace. "No," said Jesus in essence, "if they keep quiet, the stones themselves will cry out" (v. 40).

As the group drew closer to Jerusalem, Jesus wept audibly over the city, shedding bitter tears for those who would not believe in Him and for the city's future destruction by the Romans, the destruction that would take place forty years later, in AD 70.

When Jesus reached the temple, He was again frustrated. The moneychangers and the people selling birds and animals for sacrifice made its large outer court, known as the Court of the Gentiles, look like a mall or supermarket rather than a place of prayer. Moneychangers were necessary because some people had only Roman coins, and temple authorities demanded the offerings to be paid in Jewish ("temple") money. The moneychangers probably charged an unfair exchange rate and kept the profit for themselves. No wonder Jesus called the place a "den of robbers."

Bible scholars believe the moneychangers committed other atrocities too, especially in regard to the animals needed for sacrifice. Some people found it easier to buy the required sacrifices when they arrived in Jerusalem, rather than bring them all the way from home, so they appreciated having sacrificial animals available for purchase. However, the prices were often exorbitant. It is also likely that some temple leaders took advantage of the requirement that sacrificial animals had to be perfect. To ensure this, they themselves inspected the animals brought by worshipers. If they found even an almost imperceptible defect, they would reject the animal as unacceptable. Then the worshiper would be forced to buy an expensive replacement.[57]

All this angered our Lord, but more confrontations were to come. As He continued teaching at the temple each day during the week of His crucifixion, the chief priests, teachers of the Law, and other authorities continued their plots to kill Him (Luke 19:47–48). It didn't help when Jesus criticized them for their ostentatious flowing robes, their desire for important seats at banquets, their long, showy prayers, and their rules that "devoured" widows' houses. At one point, Jesus' enemies challenged His authority to teach, bringing questions intended to entangle Him in His own words. Cleverly, Jesus turned the tables, asking them a question they refused to answer, thus silencing them for the moment.

As the challenges continued, Jesus told a parable about vineyard tenants who refused to give the portion of their produce due to the owner's representatives as rent (Luke 20:9–18). Instead, these tenants plotted to take over the vineyard for themselves. Realizing that Jesus was describing them, the chief priests looked for a way to arrest Him immediately. However, because they feared the people and many of the people thought highly of Jesus, the religious rulers chose instead to challenge Him about paying taxes to Caesar and subsequently about the resurrection and marriage.

Yet, after all this, Jesus took notice of a simple widow. And because Jesus noticed her, we, too, remember her and marvel at her generosity and her trust in the Lord.

The widow's offering of two "mites" has inspired many and led to the establishment of "cent" or "mite" societies in many Christian churches during the early 1800s. In 1881, Woman's Mission to Woman, a Baptist organization, developed the first "mite box," a garnet-colored box with the name of the group in shining gold letters on its side. Soon women of other denominations were doing the same to collect coins for missions. Just as the Lord viewed the widow's gift as significant, so, too, He has blessed the pennies, nickels, and dimes countless women have placed in mite boxes. The Lutheran Women's Missionary League, for example, has raised millions of dollars through mite box contributions. These have funded hospitals, schools, and new mission efforts at home and abroad.

Not only has the Lord blessed the "mites" brought by His daughters, but He has also protected them, as an Arkansas woman discovered after a tornado. Inside her wet, damaged house surrounded by fallen trees stood her cardboard mite box, filled with coins, right on the dresser where she had left it. The water-soaked box had collapsed, but it collapsed around the coins, and not a penny was lost![58]

Scripture has much to say about God's attitude toward giving. Some experts estimate that more than two thousand verses of the Bible deal with money and possessions. One of the most familiar tells us that "God loves a cheerful giver" (2 Corinthians 9:7). The Lord also says, "Everyone to whom much was given, of him much will be required, and from him to whom they entrusted much, they will demand more" (Luke 12:48).

Everything we have belongs to our Lord. Psalm 24:1 tells us, "The earth is the LORD's, and the fullness thereof, the world and those who dwell therein." Leviticus 25:23 confirms this: "The land is Mine. For you are strangers and sojourners with Me." In Psalm 50:10, the Lord reminds us, "Every beast of the forest is Mine, the cattle on a thousand hills."

Without Him, we would have nothing. We owe Him everything, but He asks us to return only a portion. Nevertheless, it would be wrong to consider Scripture as primarily a treatise about finances. Far from being a book of rules and regulations focused on how to live life here on earth, instead, it describes what God has done down through history to secure our salvation!

Nevertheless, Scripture does say much about money, perhaps because that often is our weakest spot. We tend to worship money, trusting it as our ultimate security, forgetting that greed is idolatry (Colossians 3:5). When we hold on to our possessions with a tight fist, we betray our real values despite ten thousand words claiming to love and trust God above everything else. When children are asked to share, they often refuse, shouting, "It's mine, it's mine!" Remember making popcorn for a children's party? After a few minutes, the bowl stands empty, with none left for you! And you paid for the popcorn and popped it for them!

That's often the kind of thoughtless thanklessness we show our Lord. He gives and gives while we squeeze every cent before putting it into the offering plate.

The earliest people on earth showed their thankfulness to God by offering sacrifices. Cain gave crops from the land, and Abel offered the prized fatty portions of some of the firstborn of his flock (Genesis 4:3–4).

Later, the Mosaic Law required specific sacrifices and named the animals and plant products that could be used for sacrifices in certain cases. Those rules are recorded in the first five books of the Old Testament, especially Leviticus 1–7.

Three kinds of sacrifices were outlined: unbloody (firstfruits of crops and tithes), meat and drink offerings, and incense. With the construction of the tabernacle and, later, Solomon's temple, a central sanctuary was established. The sacrificial system then included offerings by individuals as well as offerings on behalf of the nation. Morning and evening, the priests offered daily sacrifices. Additional offerings were made each Sabbath and at the time of the new moon. During the major festivals, even more extensive sacrifices were offered.

In addition to the required offerings, the people brought "freewill offerings." As 2 Chronicles 31:5 tells us, "The people of Israel gave in abundance the firstfruits of grain, wine, oil, honey, and of all the produce of the field. And they brought in abundantly the tithe of everything." Their goal was to give the best of everything for God.

What a blessing that Christ came, offering Himself once upon the cross for all sins of all time (Hebrews 10:10, 12)! What a blessing that we are not required to bring live animals to our churches, that we don't kill and burn them on altars there! What a blessing that our pastors don't have to sprinkle blood on the four corners of our altar. What a blessing that as we partake in Holy Communion, we remember Christ's great sacrifice in offering Himself in love for us, and that in the Sacrament, we receive His very own body and blood and, by means of it, God's full and free forgiveness for all our sins.

And what a blessing that we can show our appreciation for all Christ has done for us by giving sacrificially of our time, talents, and treasure. There is so much yet to be accomplished in His name! We live in an era in which the differences between the "haves" and the "have-nots" seem to increase daily. How can we be the Body of Christ in service to the needy? One pastor tells of taking a bag of groceries to a woman living in one room with only sparse furnishings and one burner for cooking. She greeted him with the words "God is so good—He always provides for me!"

How many of us daily acknowledge the same in our much better circumstances? How many of us search for the causes of today's injustices and work to help remedy them, rather than criticizing and ostracizing those like the persistent widow who struggle to obtain justice?

Yes, Jesus personifies love and justice and compassion. He died for our shallowness and for our lack of concern toward the needy and less fortunate. He meets our needs in such generous abundance. And now, so blessed, we look for ways to become a blessing. As we rely on His love, we receive His strength through the means He has given us—His Word, Baptism, and Holy Communion. Walking in that strength, then, we find great joy as we "learn to do good; seek justice, correct oppression; bring justice to the fatherless, [and] plead the widow's cause" (Isaiah 1:17). What a great Savior we have!

The Heart of Jesus as Shown
in the Lives of Three Women in These Passages

Jesus cares about each of us and understands all our needs. In response to His merciful love, which is present in every one of life's circumstances, Jesus asks us to follow His example by seeking the lost, working for justice, and giving generously of our time, talents, and treasures in His name.

The Women Who Mourned Jesus' Death

Faithful Followers, Dutiful Caretakers
Luke 23:26–31, 49, 55–56

As they led Him away, . . . there followed Him a great multitude of the people and of women who were mourning and lamenting for Him. But turning to them Jesus said, "Daughters of Jerusalem, do not weep for Me, but weep for yourselves and for your children. For behold, the days are coming when they will say, 'Blessed are the barren and the wombs that never bore and the breasts that never nursed!'" Luke 23:26–29

[As He died,] the women who had followed Him from Galilee stood at a distance watching these things. . . . [They] followed and saw the tomb and how His body was laid. Then they returned and prepared spices and ointments. On the Sabbath they rested according to the commandment. Luke 23:49, 55–56

One Good Friday, I sat in on a Bible class for adult women at Bethesda Lutheran Home. The teacher showed the students a crucifix with a body of Christ on the cross. Approaching each class member individually, she held out the crucifix, saying, "Jesus died on the cross for my sins. Jesus died on the cross for your sins." Most looked and nodded. One woman, however, was so visibly moved by the teacher's words that she reached out to stroke the lifeless body of Christ. Then she let out the biggest sob I have ever heard.

As I listened to her weep for her sins and for what Christ endured to pay for them, I found myself wondering if Christ's death had ever affected me that deeply. Do I— and do you—today realize what He suffered for us? Do we comprehend the compassion that moved the Son of God to die such a cruel death, to give His life for others, for you and me, so we can live forever? Do we appreciate in even the smallest way the love of God the Father who sacrificed His only Son so that all who believe can be sure they will live eternally with our Lord in heaven?

The Agony of Crucifixion

Crucifixion is a horrible way to die. In English, the word *crucifixion* shares the same root as the word *excruciating*. Standing beneath the cross on Good Friday afternoon must have been just that—excruciating. I know I could never have borne it, standing there as Mary did, watching my son agonize in this way. Yet, neither could I have abandoned him to die alone. What a dilemma for Mary and for the other women who faithfully endured that terrible scene because they cared so much!

Perhaps it doesn't affect us as deeply today because we know the end of the story. Those women did not. They did not understand His promise to rise again. So far as we know, they didn't even remember it!

Historians say that family and friends usually remained at the site of execution until the accused was dead. However, in this instance, most of the male disciples failed to come, possibly because they feared being considered allies of Jesus. Perhaps they worried that they themselves would be accused of treason, just as Jesus had been. Were they in danger of being considered accomplices? Likely so. But the women stayed, weeping and horrified, to the very end. They saw and heard it all:

- *The stains on Jesus' face, left there by the drops of blood that mingled with His sweat in Gethsemane. This condition, hematidrosis, occurs under extreme stress when tiny capillaries in the sweat glands break.*

- *The false accusations by Jewish religious leaders.*

- *The crowd clamoring for the release of Barabbas, a well-known outlaw who had been imprisoned for insurrection and murder (Luke 23:19). The name* Barabbas *in Aramaic is a compound word, deriving from* bar, *meaning "son," and* abba, *meaning "father." Ironically, when the crowd called for the release of Barabbas, they were actually demanding that Pilate "release the son of the father," an apt description of Jesus—the "Son of the Father."*

- *The mockery by the guards, who also spit on Jesus (an extreme insult in that culture), struck Him in the face, put a stick (to represent a scepter) in His right hand, and pretended to worship Him.*

- *The blood oozing from Jesus' shoulders as a result of the beating ordered by Pilate. Jewish law prohibited more than forty lashes, but the Romans may have administered more. They used a whip of leather thongs with lead balls knotted into the ends. As the blows cut the skin, blood would begin oozing from the victim's body and later would attract irritating insects. So severe were these beatings that victims often died before they could be crucified.*

- *Christ's struggle to carry the heavy crossbar on His wounded shoulders until Simon of Cyrene relieved Him of His burden. Some have estimated the weight of the crossbar was anywhere from 75 to 125 pounds. The upright portion of the cross was most likely planted permanently in the ground at the site of the crucifixion. Normally the Romans chose a very public location along a major thoroughfare. They wanted crucifixions to serve as a deterrent to those tempted to commit crimes dangerous to the state—treason, rebellion, sedition. Matthew, Luke, and John do not specify the crimes of the two men crucified with Christ, but Mark 15:27 identifies them as "robbers."*

- *The words of warning uttered by Jesus to the crowd that followed Him to Calvary. In the procession were a large number of women who wailed, beating their breasts.*

Jesus turned to the women and advised, "Daughters of Jerusalem, do not weep for Me, but weep for yourselves and for your children. For behold, the days are coming when they will say, 'Blessed are the barren and the wombs that never bore and the breasts that never nursed!' Then they will begin to say to the mountains, 'Fall on us,' and to the hills, 'Cover us.' For if they do these things when the wood is green, what will happen when it is dry?" (Luke 23:28–31; compare Hosea 10:8). In other words, "Be thankful you don't have children who will suffer this way. If this can be done to an innocent man in a time of peace, what atrocities will be committed in times of war against those who refuse to repent?"

This final warning is an expression of Christ's compassion. The most widely accepted interpretation is that Jesus was looking ahead to the Roman destruction of Jerusalem in AD 66–70. The Jewish historian Josephus writes that the Roman siege of Jerusalem resulted in a famine so severe that some mothers ate their own children. (See Leviticus 26:29.) No wonder Jesus had mourned so deeply over Jerusalem five days earlier as He entered the city to celebrate the Passover (Luke 19:41).

The women who accompanied Jesus to Calvary saw and heard even more:

- *The mockery of the soldiers who dressed Jesus in a kingly red cloak and crown of thorns and, at Calvary, His humiliation in being stripped to hang naked in full sight of everyone who passed by.*

- *The soldiers dividing His garments among themselves and drawing lots for His one-piece, seamless tunic.*

- *The sound of the heavy, square, hand-wrought nails being pounded through His hands and feet. How the women must have winced at each blow of the hammer! Most authorities believe the nails were inserted between the two bones of a condemned prisoner's wrists; the wrists were considered part of the hand. The weight of a body would likely rip the nails through the palms in a matter of minutes.*

- *The sign "Jesus of Nazareth, the King of the Jews," written in Aramaic, Latin, and Greek, being nailed near the top of the cross. Such signs indicated the offense of the accused.*

- *Jesus' refusal of a sedative (gall and myrrh mixed into a cup of wine vinegar) to deaden the pain, an indication of His willingness to suffer the full pun-*

ishment for sin in our place.

- *The public shouts for Christ's crucifixion and the sneers of the Jewish leaders as He hung, suffering, on the cross. "Save Yourself!" they taunted. "He saved others, but He cannot save Himself," onlookers said to one another. One of the condemned criminals joined in: "Are You not the Christ? Save Yourself and us!" (Luke 23:39).*

- *The nerve pain, muscle cramps, and breathing difficulties Jesus endured. All accompany crucifixion, and the breathing difficulties usually cause death by asphyxiation.*

- *The eerie darkness that covered the land from noon until 3 p.m. To the people of that day, darkness was an evil omen, whether caused by an eclipse or some other phenomenon. It reminded the Jews of the ninth plague to strike Egypt, when darkness covered the land for three days and was so thick that people had to feel their way around their own homes (Exodus 10:21–22).*

- *Christ's tremendous compassion for others while He suffered for the sins of all humanity. How hard it must have been for Him to see His mother and other followers grieving for Him, heartbroken in their anguish because they still didn't understand who He was and what He had come to do. At the first Passover, the blood of a lamb on the doorframes had saved the Israelites' oldest sons. Now this oldest Son was shedding His blood as the final Passover Lamb, slain to save the lives of all believers from the beginning of creation to the end of time.*

Despite His pain, Christ Jesus continued to think of and care for others. How the four women standing at the foot of the cross must have ached as they saw Him periodically push Himself up to gasp for breath and then speak seven sentences of comfort, compassion, and forgiveness—for their benefit and for ours.

Our Lord's first words from the cross were a prayer: "Father, forgive them, for they know not what they do" (Luke 23:34). For the Roman soldiers, the religious rulers, and all the others who had taken an active role in condemning Him to death, Jesus asked God the Father for forgiveness. How many of us could have prayed that? How many of us offer forgiveness to the drunken driver who injures or kills a friend or relative? How many of us readily forgive those who lie about us or cheat us? I recently attended the funeral of my daughter-in-law, Cheryl. A friend of hers wept throughout the entire service. Afterward, she told me, "I have such guilt." She and Cheryl had had a disagreement many months before and had not spoken in more than a year. Now it was too late. I urged her to take her guilt to the cross, and I assured her she would find forgiveness there and peace because of what Jesus did for us.

Christ directed His second statement to the repentant criminal hanging on one of the two crosses adjoining His own. In response to his request, "Jesus, remember me when You come into Your kingdom," our Lord promised, "I tell you the truth, today you will be with Me in paradise." What a moving moment for the women standing beneath the crosses, watching Jesus suffer and die. Jesus had come to bring forgiveness and salvation for all, even those society considers the "worst" of sinners.

"Today you will be with Me in paradise!" We, too, cling to that assurance as we face death—our own or that of our loved ones. Christ willingly gave His life so that all who believe will be saved. Scripture repeats that truth again and again. For example, Acts 2:21 promises, "Everyone who calls upon the name of the Lord shall be saved"; and Acts 16:31 emphasizes, "Believe in the Lord Jesus, and you will be saved."

It seems so simple—so simple that we perhaps doubt its truth. Surely God requires us to *do something* to make amends for all our sins! Surely we must suffer in some way for the lies we have told, for the good deeds we have neglected, for the mistakes we have made and the disobedience in which we have willfully engaged. But Scripture is clear. There is nothing we can do, no offering we can bring, no sacrifice we can make. Only the perfect sacrifice of God's only Son could accomplish salvation for sinful human beings. In sacrificing Himself, Jesus did everything necessary. Only He lived a perfect life in our place here on earth. Only He died the perfect death we could not die in full payment for our sins. Only that death is the payment acceptable to the Father, now and forever.

The third time Christ spoke, He provided for the earthly welfare of His mother. Seeing Mary standing there at the foot of the cross, watching as the "sword" of which Simeon had spoken now pierced her soul, Jesus nodded toward John, "the disciple whom He loved," and said, "Woman, behold, your son!" Then, addressing John, He said, "Behold, your mother!" John himself tells us in his Gospel that "from that hour the disciple took her to his own home" (John 19:26–27). Jesus thus completed His earthly obligation as the oldest son in the family by providing for Mary's care.

The Roman Catholic Church uses this exchange as proof that Mary lived as a perpetual virgin, bearing no other children. The reformer, Martin Luther, also accepted this traditional view. If Mary had had other children, wouldn't they have cared for her? Christians of other denominations, however, take the various scriptural references to Jesus' half-brothers and half-sisters literally. They believe that although Mary had no sexual relations with Joseph until after the birth of Christ (Matthew 1:16, 24–25), the couple did subsequently have other children. Consequently, the other brothers should have taken responsibility for Mary. Most Protestant scholars believe Jesus gave that responsibility to John because His brothers did not accept His divinity until after the resurrection, and Jesus wanted to ensure compatible surroundings for Mary in the hours and days that followed His death and resurrection.

Christ's fourth statement, sometimes called the "cry of dereliction," echoed the words of Psalm 22:1. The words confused the onlookers: *"Eli, Eli, lema sabachthani?"* Translated, this sentence means, "My God, my God, why have You forsaken Me?" (Matthew 27:46). However, some observers misunderstood, thinking Jesus was calling for help from Elijah. Because Elijah was taken up into heaven without dying (2 Kings 2:1–12), some people at that time believed that God sometimes sent Elijah to rescue the faithful from trouble, in a way similar to the manner in which He uses angels to minister to His people.[59]

The significance of Christ's outcry is explained by Paul E. Kretzmann: "Forsaken, rejected by God: that is the torture of hell. What deep humiliation for the eternal Son of God to enter into the depths of everlasting death and torment! But, by His enduring the torments of hell, we have been liberated, for in the midst of this most terrible Passion He remained obedient to God and thus conquered wrath, hell and damnation for us."[60]

In His fifth word from the cross, Jesus gave evidence of His human nature. In fulfillment of the Old Testament prophesy "For my thirst they gave me sour wine to drink" (Psalm 69:21), Jesus said simply, "I thirst" (John 19:28). The soldiers guarding the scene had wine vinegar mixed with water nearby for their own use, so they soaked a sponge in their jug and, using a long stalk of hyssop, lifted the sponge to Jesus' lips.

In His sixth utterance, perhaps the most dramatic one of all, our Lord declared victory. He cried out in a loud voice, "It is finished!" His saving work was done! His mission of redemption was complete!

He then spoke His final words, "Father, into Your hands I commit My spirit!" (Luke 23:46). Then He bowed His head and died.

As difficult as it is for us to imagine all this, we know that Christ went to the cross on our behalf and in our place. We, by our own sinfulness, made it necessary. God, by His own unfathomable love, made it possible. Jesus was betrayed, convicted, and crucified for our sins—all this because we are God's beloved daughters. We did nothing and could do nothing to save ourselves. God Himself did it all!

Death and Burial

The Friday Jesus died was no ordinary day. This Friday was a day of preparation, not only for the Sabbath that began at sundown, but also for the Passover Festival that was to be celebrated simultaneously. For both reasons, the Jewish religious leaders wanted the bodies removed from their crosses before the day ended. (See Deuteronomy 21:22–23.) Under normal circumstances, the Romans would have insisted that the bodies be left on the crosses to rot for several days before burying them in a common grave. But to appease the Jews, the guards set out to hasten the deaths of the crucified men by breaking their legs. They did so first to the two criminals hanging on either side of Jesus. This made it impossible for them to push their bodies up to breathe, and they died more quickly. Had this measure not been taken, death might not have come for several days.

However, when the soldiers came to Jesus' body, they saw He was dead already. They didn't bother to break His legs, thus fulfilling Numbers 9:12 and Psalm 34:20. Still, to make sure He really had died and had not simply fainted, one of the soldiers thrust a spear into Jesus' side, possibly nicking His heart or a major artery. Many have commented on the blood and water that flowed from the wound made by the soldier's spear (John 19:34).[61] Several hymns also mention this detail. Regardless of its physical cause, we see in the blood, cleansing from sin, and in the water, the new life God the Holy Spirit offers (John 7:38–39).

Yes, Jesus was dead. It had taken just six hours! The agonizing vigil of the women at the foot of the cross was mercifully ended. Their grief would go on . . . but only until Sunday morning.

Lest anyone doubt Jesus' identity, God the Father added His exclamation mark to the event. As our Lord gave up His spirit into the Father's hands, an earthquake rumbled across the land. The curtain in the temple that separated the Holy Place from the Most Holy Place ripped in two, opening the way into God's holy presence. Many saints were raised from death as well:

> *The curtain of the temple was torn in two, from top to bottom. And the earth shook, and the rocks were split. The tombs also were opened. And many bodies of the saints who had fallen asleep were raised, and coming out of the tombs after His resurrection they went into the holy city and appeared to many. Matthew 27:51–53*

The observers, including one of Christ's Gentile executioners, were overcome with terror. He exclaimed, "Surely He was the Son of God!" Bible scholars disagree on what exactly the centurion meant. Was he only attributing the supposed power of his Greek or Romans gods to the One he had just executed? Or did he somehow understand that Jesus is the world's Savior and as a result, had come to true faith? Let's hope it was the latter.

The tearing of the temple curtain carries great significance for us still today. It separated the Holy Place, where Zechariah and the other priests burned incense on a daily basis, from the Holy of Holies, considered the throne room of God and visited only by Israel's high priest—and that only once a year.

This curtain was about four inches thick, thirty-three feet wide, and sixty-six feet high. It weighed between four and six tons and, if we believe what the Talmud reports, it required three hundred priests to carry it.[62] Josephus tells us it was embroidered with threads of four colors: fine linen (ivory or tan), blue, scarlet, and purple. For a curtain of such proportions to rip in two required nothing less than the hand of God!

That it happened and how it happened matter much less than *why* it happened. What did it mean? The barrier of separation between a holy God and sinful human beings had been removed—and by our Lord Himself. No longer must we rely on an earthly intermediary to gain access to God's mercy on our behalf. Jesus Himself has become our high priest. No sacrifice beyond His own is necessary.

Additionally, Christ's death established "the priesthood of all believers." We can come directly to the Lord in repentance and faith, trusting Him to hear, forgive, and help. And we can intercede for the needs of others too (James 5:16). The way into God's presence is open, and He invites us to come to Him freely.

Joseph of Arimathea and Nicodemus took Jesus' body down from the cross and buried it. Joseph was a disciple, "but secretly for fear of the Jews" (John 19:38). Nevertheless, he was a believer, waiting for the kingdom of God. He had not consented to Christ's crucifixion when the matter came before the Jewish High Council, the Sanhedrin. Evidently, Joseph had enough power or money to demand and attain an immediate audience with Pilate and secure possession of Jesus' body. Joseph brought clean linen to modestly and respectfully cover Christ's naked form and serve as His grave clothing.

Three years or so earlier, Nicodemus, another member of the Sanhedrin, had come to Jesus at night. Jesus graciously received him and taught him about his need to be born again (John 3:1–21). Now, Nicodemus brought a seventy-five-pound mixture of myrrh and aloes with which he intended to begin the burial process for the Lord's body.

Together the two men wrapped the corpse in the linen, binding in the spices in accordance with Jewish burial customs. Then they placed the body in Joseph's own new tomb, a tomb that had been cut out of the rock in a garden near the crucifixion site (Matthew 27:60; John 19:41). Finally the men rolled a stone in front of the entrance to protect it from animals and intruders. To make sure no one stole the body and at the requests of the chief priests and Pharisees, Pilate had the entrance sealed and posted a guard (Matthew 27:65–66).

Women Were There!

Mary Magdalene and Mary the mother of Joses followed Joseph and Nicodemus, eager to see where they buried Jesus' body. Then, Luke tells us, they went home

immediately to prepare more spices and perfumed ointments, intending to return and provide a more proper
burial according to Jewish tradition. However, since the
Sabbath began when the sun went down, the women
rested on Saturday as the commandment required.

The two Marys were not the only women to witness
Christ's crucifixion. Luke 23:55 talks about the "women
who had come with [Jesus] from Galilee." Mark 15:41 tells
us there were many of them. Some watched from a distance, and a few stayed close to the cross. Other Gospel
writers list the more prominent witnesses:

- *Mary Magdalene*

- *Mary the mother of Joses and James the younger
  (Jesus had two disciples named James)*

- *Salome (probably the mother of Zebedee's sons,
  James and John)*

- *Mary, Jesus' mother*

- *Mary's sister*

Because Matthew, Mark, and Luke use different descriptions, Bible students have often puzzled over precisely
who the women were. Although the specifics and relationships would surely be interesting, it doesn't really matter. What does matter is that these women cared deeply
enough to follow Jesus all the way from Galilee to Judea
and to stay with Him as He died. Because they truly believed in Him, they were willing to use their time and energy to assist His cause and to support His mission. What a
privilege they had as eyewitnesses to His life, ministry, and
death—and then, of course, to His resurrection, as we shall
see in the next chapter.

Faithful to the end, they stayed at Golgotha, "the place
of the skull," for long, exhausting hours, remaining with

the Lord until He died. A few, as we have seen, followed His body to the grave. Despite their fear of the Romans and the taunts of the crowd, they did not deny Him. Despite their aching hearts, they remained resolutely at the crucifixion site, grieving for Jesus, weeping over His suffering, and mourning for their own loss.

How hard this all must have been for Mary, Jesus' mother. As she awaited His death, did she remember the annunciation message Gabriel had delivered and the miracle of her pregnancy all those years ago? Did she recall Simeon's words to her in the temple as she cradled baby Jesus in her arms and tried to take in his prophecy that a sword would pierce her heart? Now it was happening, just as surely as the soldier's sword pierced Jesus' side.

Did she understand that He had to die to save the world? We don't know. But no mother is ever prepared for her child to die, regardless of the circumstance. How numb, how heartbroken Mary must have felt as she turned from that cross, believing she would never see Him again. How she must have tossed and turned as she tried to sleep that night. As darkness fell, as the Sabbath and the Passover festival began, as everyone began to celebrate once again God's deliverance of His people from Egypt, surely Mary must have wondered: Why had God not delivered her son, His Son conceived by the Holy Spirit, from this horrible fate?

Yet, as a believer and follower of Jesus herself, Mary would have known the prayer He taught His disciples. She would have known the Third Petition, "Thy will be done on earth as it is in heaven." Perhaps she even prayed it that night. How hard it is for us to understand God's will when we are hurting or have suffered a loss! The onlookers at Calvary wailed and beat their breasts to show their sorrow. When we grieve, we, too, need to express our pain. Keeping it inside can only raise our stress level. If we experience feelings of guilt, we can and should confess them to the

Lord. Sometimes we may find it helpful to share them with our pastor too, and perhaps even with a trusted counselor. Whatever lies behind our guilt, we can know that in Christ, God always forgives His repentant children!

In the midst of grief, then, we need to find friends who are willing to listen and weep with us. When my husband died, a friend with whom I had worked in our local Women's Missionary League welcomed my calls at any time of the day or evening. Years later, when my daughter died, a friend in my neighborhood said, "I have trouble sleeping. Call me anytime—I'll probably be awake."

It is also important to have friends who hug and who provide other kinds of physical support. We all need the touch of other human beings, especially in times of loss. During a talk I gave on dealing with grief some months after my husband's death, I mentioned the importance of touch. Someone in the audience reminded me of the Scripture verse in which the Lord promises to be the "husband" of the widow (Isaiah 54:5). Certainly, our relationship with the Lord is important; certainly, we can cling to His promises. Yet, He created us as physical beings, beings who need the touch and the companionship of other human beings. We need not deny this, nor is it healthy to do so.

Nevertheless, God's Word provides the ultimate solace and consolation. Among the verses I have found most helpful are these:

- *Let not your hearts be troubled. Believe in God; believe also in Me. In My Father's house are many rooms. If it were not so, would I have told you that I go to prepare a place for you? And if I go and prepare a place for you, I will come again and will take you to Myself, that where I am you may be also. John 14:1–3*

- *Jesus said to [Martha], "I am the resurrection and the life. Whoever believes in Me, though he die, yet* shall he live, and everyone who lives and believes in Me shall never die." John 11:25–26

- *For me to live is Christ, and to die is gain. Philippians 1:21*

- *Blessed be the God and Father of our Lord Jesus Christ, the Father of mercies and God of all comfort, who comforts us in all our affliction, so that we may be able to comfort those who are in any affliction, with the comfort with which we ourselves are comforted by God. For as we share abundantly in Christ's sufferings, so through Christ we share abundantly in comfort too. 2 Corinthians 1:3–5*

- *His favor is for a lifetime. Weeping may tarry for the night, but joy comes with the morning. Psalm 30:5*

- *We know that for those who love God all things work together for good. Romans 8:28*

In times of loss, it's often hard to believe that God is working in the situation for our good. Yet many Christians will testify to the truth of Romans 8:28. We simply do not know how much suffering God prevented by taking our loved one when He did. We do not know what other tragedies might have occurred had he or she lived. The Lord, however, knows everything, and He works in every circumstance for our ultimate good.

Recognizing the truth of these Scriptures, we can celebrate each Christian life and death. Just as Jesus' death meant His work was complete and our salvation had been won, our death means eternal joy with Christ. That is life's ultimate purpose and goal.

We have been baptized into Christ's death—and, therefore, into His life (Romans 6:3–11). We have died and been raised with Him. The "second death," eternal death, will never harm us. When Satan rages, accuses, and tries to terrify us, we need not fear. We belong to Jesus in life and death. He has sealed us as His own by water and the Word. We rest, then, in His promise: "Though you do not now see Him, you believe in Him and rejoice with joy that is inexpressible and filled with glory" (1 Peter 1:8).

The Heart of Jesus as Shown in the Lives of the Women at the Crucifixion

Jesus loved us so much that He willingly laid down His life so we could live with Him eternally. When we mourn the death of loved ones, we can remember Jesus' care. And we can, in courage, continue the remaining work He has for us to do here on earth.

Chapter
TWELVE

The Women Who Rejoiced in Jesus' Resurrection

Rejoicing Saints, Encouraged Evangelists
Luke 24:1–12

On the first day of the week, at early dawn, they went to the tomb, taking the spices they had prepared. . . . Behold, two men stood by them in dazzling apparel. . . . The men said to them, "Why do you seek the living among the dead? He is not here, but has risen." . . . Returning from the tomb they told all these things to the eleven and to all the rest. Now it was Mary Magdalene and Joanna and Mary the mother of James and the other women with them who told these things to the apostles, but these words seemed to them an idle tale, and they did not believe them. Luke 24:1, 4–6, 9–11

For Christians, *Easter* and *joy* are synonymous. "Christ the Lord is risen today," we sing, with its multiple alleluias.

The most joyous Easter celebration I ever attended occurred during a visit to Japan a few years ago. Friends met us at our Tokyo hotel and then took us by train and Metro (subway) to a large high school that a Christian congregation had rented for its Easter worship services. Their own church building would not hold the crowds that were expected.

As we came out of the Metro station, a group was standing on the corner with festive balloons and a sign pointing the way to "Easter service." We walked two blocks as directed, and at that corner, another group stood with balloons and another sign, this time indicating a turn to the left.

As we continued walking, we saw people returning from the 8 a.m. service. When they met us, they would call out, "Christ is risen!" We and others walking toward the school would respond with "Hallelujah!" or "He is risen indeed!" In a few minutes, we reached the large auditorium. Before long, it was completely filled for the 10 a.m. service.

And what a service it was! A jubilant children's choir. A lively teen choir. A huge choir of adults, with the men dressed in formal attire and the women in long black skirts and sparkly sequined tops. They were wearing their best for the Lord. They sang. We sang. Young people presented a drama. The pastor preached twice—both times in English, with the Japanese translation projected on a screen. Everyone prayed, and we all sang some more. How thankful we were that God raised Christ from the dead, that our sins are gone, and that in Jesus, we have the gift of eternal life. As we left the building, there were more shouts of "Christ is risen!" It was a joyous day indeed.

Japanese Christians are dedicated to outreach. When I visited the Tokyo Lutheran Center, I learned that both an international congregation and a Japanese congregation hold Sunday services there. Because Tokyo is so large, it takes a long time for some people to travel to church, so the entire day is dedicated to the Lord. After worship, the women prepare lunch at the center two Sundays a month, and on the other Sundays, people divide into groups to eat at nearby restaurants. Then they return to the center for Bible study, fellowship, and meetings that continue throughout the afternoon.

They also told me about another Lutheran church out-side of Tokyo that was facing the same problem as many congregations in the United States—difficulty in attract-ing young people. In fact, that church had no children in its Sunday School; but they prayed hard, and they firmly believed the Lord would soon send children. To be ready for that day, four adults came every Sunday and taught the lesson to one another so they were prepared.

How many of us in the United States would be that faithful, that trusting? How happily would we spend all day Sunday at church or station people on street corners to direct worshipers to our Easter service?

The women who returned to Christ's tomb on the first Resurrection Sunday morning had that kind of dedication. Despite all they had endured at the foot of the cross on the first Good Friday, they remained faithful. Determined to anoint Christ's body as required by Jewish custom, to do even more than Joseph and Nicodemus had done, they made their way to the tomb as morning dawned.

He Is Risen!

At some point, the women purchased additional spices and perfumes—either just before the Sabbath began at sundown on Friday or when it ended on Saturday at sundown. They kept the Sabbath faithfully, but very early on Sunday morning, they were on their way to the garden where Joseph's tomb was located.

Again we could ask the "who" question, because each Gospel writer describes the women in different terms. Luke (24:10) tells us that Mary Magdalene, Joanna, Mary the mother of James, and others went together. All four Gospel writers consistently identify Mary Magdalene as being at the tomb. The differences in the accounts should not surprise us. Each writer focused on different aspects of the event and on different individuals participating in each part of the whole event. Depending on the point of view the writers took and the focus each writer wanted to emphasize, the characters singled out for special attention would naturally differ.

Although we assume the women at the tomb had heard Jesus' preaching and had seen His miracles, none of them expected what they found that morning. Yes, Jesus had raised people from the dead, just as several Old Testament prophets had. But no one had ever raised himself! Although Jesus had clearly told His followers that He would rise again, such a possibility lay beyond their comprehension.

As the women approached the tomb, their worries were more mundane: "Who will roll away the stone for us from the entrance of the tomb?" (Mark 16:3). Opening a tomb so soon after a burial was unusual in itself. Under normal conditions, no one entered a sealed tomb until at least a year later—when the bones of the deceased would be gathered and placed in an ossuary—and perhaps not until another member of the family died and was buried. Opening a tomb sealed by a large stone would take at least two strong men. In their urgency to complete the burial process, the women had evidently forgotten this practical matter until they were well on their way to Joseph's garden tomb.

The women soon saw their concern was unfounded; the entrance stood wide open. The large round stone had already been rolled aside. The surprise soon disappeared as a wave of shock passed over them. When the women looked inside the tomb, the Lord's body was gone! In yet another mind-numbing blow, suddenly two men appeared in the dimness of the tomb—angels dressed in white robes that gleamed and flashed like lightning, scattering the darkness!

Trembling with fright, the women bowed with their faces to the ground. "Why do you seek the living among the dead?" one angel asked (Luke 24:5), reminding them of what Jesus had promised. At these words, the women remembered. They began to realize what Christ had meant. Could He be alive? The angel commanded them to deliver that message to the other disciples! Yes, Jesus had risen, just as He said. Who would believe it? Who would believe them? Afraid, and anxious to reach the disciples, they spoke to no one along the way back into the city.

They arrived to find a group of their friends, disciples all, in mourning. Still grief-stricken and weeping, those who heard the report were astonished. The women's words sounded like nonsense to them, Luke tells us. Peter and John immediately took off, running to see for themselves. They were amazed when they entered the tomb and found the Lord's grave clothes neatly in place with no body inside, just as the women had said. The men left quickly, puzzled and wondering what could have happened.

Scripture tells us that later, Mary Magdalene and some of the other women returned to the tomb too. As Mary looked inside, she saw the two angels, spoke briefly with them, and then turned around to find someone standing there. She presumed He was the gardener. "Woman," He said, "why are you weeping? Whom are you seeking?"

(John 20:15). "Sir, if you have carried Him away, tell me where you have laid Him, and I will take Him away," a confused and still-perplexed Mary replied.

It was a mind-boggling moment. In one of the most extraordinary experiences in the history of world, Mary was about to be the first person to see and speak with the risen Christ!

The "gardener" said just one word—"Mary!"—and she knew. In Aramaic, she cried out ecstatically, "Rabboni!" The word means "teacher." This was Jesus! The other women knelt in worship and touched His feet (Matthew 28:9). Mary Magdalene must have reached out to hug Him. "Do not cling to Me," the glorified Jesus told her (John 20:17), explaining that He was about to return to His Father. Now risen from the dead, He would soon ascend to heaven. His time on earth as a visible, physical human being was ending. Their relationship was about to change.

Again, Mary received the directive to "Go and tell," this time from Christ Himself. She was the first to carry the message that would change the world: Jesus was *alive*! As a result, St. Augustine and other Early Church Fathers would call her "the Apostle to the Apostles."[63]

Mary did as the Lord instructed, going to the disciples with the news: "'I have seen the Lord!'—and [she told them] that He had said these things to her" (John 20:18). That evening, Christ came and stood among them, blessing them with the words "Peace be with you!" (v. 19). John's comment that "the disciples were glad when they saw the Lord" (v. 20) is undoubtedly an understatement.

Jesus' resurrection changed their lives forever! It has changed our lives too! Our joy will have no end. If Jesus had not risen, no one would remember Him today. His name would have turned to dust along with those of other insurgents who died battling the great, conquering Roman armies. Another dead preacher, another dead zealot.

But rise He did, and He proved the reality of it on Easter Sunday evening by eating a piece of fish with the disciples. Then, a week later, He answered Thomas's doubts, inviting the reluctant disciple to touch the wounds in His side and the nail marks in His hands. Doubts gave way to faith in the face of overwhelming evidence.

Jesus' resurrection proved His divine power over death. It also showed His defeat of sin. After hearing the Easter story, Oscar, a Bethesda resident, told a chapel audience, "Because of Jesus, there isn't a single sin nowhere on me!" In addition, Jesus' resurrection demonstrated His power over Satan. As Chaplain Frederick Stiemke used to tell the Bethesda residents, "Jesus went down into hell and told Satan, 'I win! You lose!'" (Colossians 2:13–15; 1 Peter 3:18–20).

Go and Tell!

It's worth repeating: Jesus' victory over sin, death, and Satan has changed our lives forever. The Lord also asks us as believers to "Go and tell!" We sometimes shy away from this task. Perhaps we worry, What if I speak to someone about Christ and they ask me a question I can't answer? What if I can't remember the best Bible texts to prove my point? What if I get mixed up and say the wrong thing? What if my friends avoid me because talking about faith makes them feel uncomfortable?

When we ask questions like those, we might also want to ask yet another question: What if we *don't* tell?

As students of the Bible, we can take courage and find comfort in the promise that the Holy Spirit will give us the words we need. The Scriptures encourage us in the privilege we have received as messengers of the Good News:

- *Having gifts that differ according to the grace given to us, let us use them: if prophecy, in proportion to our faith; if service, in our serving; the one who teaches, in his teaching; the one who exhorts, in his exhortation; the one who contributes, in generosity; the one who leads, with zeal; the one who does acts of mercy, with cheerfulness. Romans 12:6–8*

- *Go therefore and make disciples of all nations, baptizing them in the name of the Father and of the Son and of the Holy Spirit, teaching them to observe all that I have commanded you. Matthew 28:19–20*

- *Fear not, nor be afraid. . . . You are my witnesses! Is there a God besides Me? There is no Rock; I know not any. Isaiah 44:8*

- *You will be my witnesses in Jerusalem and in all Judea and Samaria, and to the ends of the earth. Acts 1:8*

When we hesitate, we can remember:

- *We don't have to be perfect to witness. The Samaritan woman whom Jesus met at the well (John 4) had had five husbands and was living with a man who was not her husband. But when she told the people in her community about Jesus, they were drawn to see for themselves, and they believed.*

- *We don't have to do it alone. The Holy Spirit is always at work in us and through us. The same Spirit who guided and strengthened the apostles lives in us today, building His Church, just as Jesus promised.*

- *We don't have to do it all. Paul speaks of a division of labor, noting that he "planted, Apollos watered, but God gave the growth" (1 Corinthians 3:6). All of God's children are engaged in the task of sharing the Gospel together. Words one person shares may* build on what someone else has said, and eventually, under God's gracious hand, the listener understands and believes.

- We don't have to speak with the eloquence of an orator, the theological insight of a pastor, or the fervor of a politician. Just a simple, personal message is often the most meaningful.

- We don't have to cite Bible verse after Bible verse. Many times, simply telling what Jesus has done in our lives and what He wants to do in the life of the listener will have a great impact. If we're too shy to share even our own experience, we can simply invite the person to a nonthreatening event at our church and help the visitor make new friends. In this world of locked doors and security complexes where many neighbors never meet one another, many people are looking for friends. What better friend than our Lord Jesus?!

- We don't have to speak in confrontational, accusatory, or stern terms. We don't need to focus pointedly on our friend's sinful nature and on the dangers of hellfire. Of course, we don't deny those realities, but it's usually helpful to start in a different place. Most people realize they make mistakes and have violated God's Law (even if they don't admit or self-protectively excuse or deny it). A recognition of this followed by a warm, loving discussion about God's love for all people, God's purpose for our lives, and the peace and joy that the Christian faith brings can make a real difference in many hearts.

- We can call in reinforcements. Many people carry tracts or Scripture excerpts to give to people who have questions about the Christian faith and who are open to learning more. We can ask permission to share our friend's name with our pastor or with *our church's outreach board. And we can pray for our friend!*

Rejoice!

When we trust in our resurrected and living Lord brings us joy! It makes us want to celebrate! It encourages and sustains us. In dozens of passages, God's Word invites us to rejoice. Here are just a few examples:

- *Glory in His holy name; let the hearts of those who seek the LORD rejoice. 1 Chronicles 16:10*

- *Be glad in the LORD, and rejoice, O righteous, and shout for joy, all you upright in heart! Psalm 32:11*

- *Let the righteous one rejoice in the LORD and take refuge in Him! Let all the upright in heart exult! Psalm 64:10*

- *Oh come, let us sing to the LORD; let us make a joyful noise to the rock of our salvation! Psalm 95:1*

- *Rejoice in the LORD, O you righteous, and give thanks to His holy name! Psalm 97:12*

- *With trumpets and the sound of the horn make a joyful noise before the King, the LORD. Psalm 98:6*

- *This is the day that the LORD has made; let us rejoice and be glad in it. Psalm 118:24*

- *Rejoice and be glad, for your reward is great in heaven. Matthew 5:12*

- *Rejoice in the Lord always; again I will say, Rejoice. Philippians 4:4*

- *Rejoice always . . . for this is the will of God in Christ Jesus for you. 1 Thessalonians 5:16, 18*

- *Let us rejoice and exult and give Him the glory. Revelation 19:7*

Because Christ has paid the debt we had incurred by our sins, we have ample cause to rejoice. Yet how often we succumb to life's difficulties, to the mood of the culture around us, or to the weakness of our own sinful flesh, allowing them to dampen our joy as we worship.

That's what Gertrude Behanna discovered when she became a Christian at age 53. A millionaire, she had been married three times, was addicted to alcohol and drugs, and had tried to commit suicide. Then friends told her about Christ. Coming to faith in Him brought indescribable joy to her heart.

How shocked she was, then, when she attended public worship for the first time. She expected the other worshipers to express the joy she felt. After all, they had known the Lord for years. Surely they would radiate His love! Instead, she discovered long faces and a mood more appropriate for a funeral. No one even spoke to her! Week after week, she attended churches in various areas, only to make the same discovery. Her wonder grew deeper as she questioned how her fellow believers could come into God's presence, week by week, and not experience the joy of resurrection that danced in the air.[64]

We know the answer, don't we? We believe the Gospel . . . we truly do. But the pressures and struggles of everyday life sometimes overwhelm our joy. The worries of family and job, of bills and investments, of injustice and misery in our world threaten to drown our peace. Satan works hard to keep the Good News of the resurrection out of our thoughts. We bury the peace of sins forgiven in a dark corner at the bottom of our hearts. Forgetfulness blocks our joy.

But this sin, too, has been washed away in the blood of the Lamb. Each new day holds out new opportunities for worship and for joyful witness. When we realize what has happened to our joy, we can confess our sins, confident that Jesus has forgiven them and will continue to cleanse us from all unrighteousness. As the Holy Spirit works in us, He restores the joy of our salvation and grants the kind of willing spirit that sustains us (Psalm 51:12).

Then we will "teach transgressors [Christ's] ways, and sinners will return to [Him]" (v. 13).

Growing in Appreciation

Rejoicing is a matter of thankfulness and of growing recognition of what the Lord has done for us. Both solemnity and exuberance have their rightful place in worship. I believe that so many of us have been Christians for so long that we forget to appreciate God's amazing love. Our faith has become routine. We forget to read Scripture daily. We forget to pray in the awesome assurance that our almighty God really does listen and respond.

But praise the Lord that He does not treat us as we deserve. He patiently forgives us, over and over again; He has sealed His forgiveness with the blood of His only Son. There is no greater love than this!

When we're inclined to doubt, then we have only to remember that hundreds of people did see Him after His resurrection and before the ascension. Scripture records at least twelve appearances—ten before the ascension and two after:

- *Jesus appeared to the women returning from the tomb (Matthew 28:9–10).*

- *Jesus appeared to the two disciples on the road to Emmaus (Luke 24:13–32).*

- *Jesus appeared to Simon Peter in Jerusalem (Luke 24:34).*

- *He appeared to His followers in the locked room in Jerusalem on Easter evening, Thomas being absent (Luke 24:36–43).*

- *Jesus appeared to the disciples eight days later, this time when Thomas was present (John 20:24–29).*

- *Jesus appeared to seven disciples on the shore of Galilee (John 21:1–24).*

- *He appeared to James (1 Corinthians 15:7).*

- *He spoke to eleven disciples on a mountain in Galilee (Matthew 28:16–20).*

- *He appeared to five hundred believers at one time (1 Corinthians 15:6).*

- *Jesus blessed many of His followers on the Mount of Olives on the day of His ascension (Luke 24:50–53).*

- *Paul met Jesus on the road to Damascus (Acts 9:3–6).*

- *Finally, Stephen looked up to heaven as he was dying; he saw both the glory of God and Jesus Himself, standing at the right hand of the Majesty on high (Acts 7:55).*

There may have been additional appearances between Christ's resurrection and ascension. Scripture says that Jesus did "many other things. . . . Were every one of them to be written, . . . the world itself could not contain the books that would be written" (John 21:25).

All these events form a convincing body of evidence that our Lord did indeed rise from death, not just somehow "spiritually," but physically and in glory. To His first-century disciples, Jesus said, "Have you believed because you have seen Me? Blessed are those who have not seen and yet have believed" (John 20:29). And believe they did! So convinced were they that Christ had risen and was ascended into heaven that they endured all sorts of hardships and challenges, beatings and imprisonment, torture, and even violent death. None of this could stop them from spreading the news of His love in regions near and far. "We cannot help speaking about what we have seen and heard!" they claimed (compare Acts 4:20).

Tradition claims that ten of the eleven original apostles died for the faith. Only John escaped, and he endured extreme hardship. (Judas, of course, had already betrayed Jesus and then committed suicide.) To be sure, Scripture does not tell us what happened to most of them. We do know that King Herod killed James the Greater in Jerusalem (Acts 12:2). It's likely that Peter and Andrew were crucified, Peter in Rome and Andrew in southern Greece after carrying the Gospel to Russia. Many believe Philip was martyred in Turkey. Matthew's martyrdom may have taken place in Ethiopia or Persia. Tradition says Bartholomew was skinned alive and then beheaded after evangelizing in the region around present-day Turkey, Iraq, and Iran. Thomas is said to have carried the Gospel to India; he was likely speared to death near Madras. Jude and Simon the Zealot were probably killed in Persia, although some say Simon died in Britain. James the Less preached in Israel and is said to have been martyred in Egypt. Matthias, who took the place of Judas Iscariot after Jesus ascended into heaven, was reportedly stoned and beheaded for the faith.

Others in addition to the Twelve endured persecution and death for the faith. James, Jesus' brother (or cousin, depending upon how one translates the word into English), remained unconvinced of Christ's deity during Jesus' three-year ministry; yet, after the Lord's resurrection and ascension, he became head of the Church in Jerusalem. Tradition says he was eventually stoned and clubbed to death. The two Gospel writers who were not among the twelve apostles may also have been martyred—Mark in Egypt and Luke in Greece.

The history of martyrdom, in and of itself, provides convincing proof of the Savior's resurrection. If Christ did not rise, surely at least one and probably all of these eye-witnesses would have recanted their testimony. Few people willingly die for a lie. People simply do not sacrifice their lives for something they do not believe to be absolutely true.

Heaven, Our Eternal Home

What about the strength of our own faith? Nehemiah 8:10 says, "The joy of the Lord is your strength." Fueling our joy is Christ's promise, "In My Father's house are many rooms; if it were not so, I would have told you. I am going there to prepare a place for you" (John 14:2). Our Savior has promised to return someday to take us to live forever with Him in heaven. His words to Martha ring in the ears of every faithful disciple today: "I am the resurrection and the life. He who believes in Me will live, even though he dies" (John 11:25). This is the heart of our Lord's message, His promise of eternal life, based on the forgiveness of sins He Himself won for us on Calvary's cross.

What a place heaven must be! Revelation 21 describes the Holy City in mind-boggling terms. God's glory itself sets the city alight. Its jewel-like brilliance, streets of pure gold, and gates of pearl set our imagination reeling. We yearn for a glimpse of the crystal-clear river flowing with the water of life through the center of the city. We long for a taste of the fruit that grows from the trees planted along that river's banks. The descriptions given in Revelation—and in other Bible books too—bear reading again and again.

Of course, the best thing about heaven is that the Lord dwells there. He will fill us with joy in His presence and with the pleasures that have awaited us at His right hand from all eternity (Psalm 16:11). There God "will wipe away every tear from [our] eyes, and death shall be no more, neither shall there be mourning, nor crying, nor pain anymore, for the former things have passed away" (Revelation 21:4).

For now, though, we live on earth. We endure the "former things," the troubles and trials that will one day pass away. Satan still assails us with doubts and torments us with the frustrations of daily living. In our current context, it seems incredible, this Gospel. Our human minds can't quite grasp it. We pray, as did the worried father in Matthew 9:24, "I do believe; help me overcome my unbelief!" God will answer prayers like these! The Holy Spirit uses His Word and the Sacraments to create and strengthen within us the faith that Jesus' resurrection is real and true. Jesus did indeed rise from the dead. Jesus did indeed conquer death, and despite our unbelief, our fears, our sins, Jesus did this *for us*!

And since He did, we, like the women at His tomb, can say, "I don't quite understand it, but it's true. I know it's true."

Just as Jesus came to encourage, empower, and transform the women who accompanied Him as He engaged in His earthly ministry, so He is with each of us today saying, "I created you. I understand your needs. I care about you. Talk with Me for I am listening. I value you, and I encourage you to grow spiritually. I forgive your sins. I want you to 'go and tell' about Me. I want you to be part of My body, serving others in My name. Believe in Me, and continue to look forward to the day when we will live together forever in heaven."

The Heart of Jesus as Shown in the Life of the Women at the Resurrection

Christ is alive and has ascended to heaven, where He has prepared a place for each of us who believe. This is the great news He wants us to "go and tell."

Endnotes

1. Edersheim, Alfred, *The Temple—Its Ministry and Services As They Were at the Time of Jesus Christ* (London: Hodder and Stoughton, 1904), www.ccel.org/ccel/edersheim/temple.html; chapter 4; 1 Chronicles 23:4–5, 28ff.

2. Josephus, *Antiquities of the Jews, Book XV*, 11, 1, trans. William Whiston (Wesley Center Online), http://wesley.nnu.edu/biblical_studies/josephus/index.htm.

3. www.localhistories.org/oldtestament.html; Home Life in Times, Arthur W. Klinck (St. Louis: CPH, 1969), 162.

4. http://www.americanbible.org/brcpages/Circumcision. Used by permission.

5. Bernstein, Rick, "Give Away the Farm," *Guideposts* magazine, June 2008, 92–95.

6. Taege, Marlys, "Me—A Mentor?" *Lutheran Woman's Quarterly,* Summer 2004, 10.

7. Keener, Craig S, *The IVP Bible Background Commentary* (Downers Grove, IL: InterVarsity Press, 1993), 193.

8. Bethlehem, the city in which the Bread of Life was born, means "House of Bread" in Hebrew.

9. Keener, op. cit., 47.

10. Franzmann, Martin H., *Concordia Self-Study Commentary* (St. Louis, MO: Concordia Publishing House, 1979), New Testament 14.

11. Beck, William F., *The Christ of the Gospels* (St. Louis, MO: Concordia Publishing House, 1959), 8.

12. Ibid, 9.

13. Maier, Paul, *Josephus, The Essential Works* (Grand Rapids, MI: Kregel Publications, 1988), 257.

14. Keener, op. cit., 268.

15. Vanosh, Miriam Feinberg, *Daily Life at the Time of Jesus* (Herzlia, Israel: Palphot Ltd., 1999), 57.

16. Ginzberg, Louis, "Asher—In Rabbinical Literature," *Jewish Encyclopedia,* 1901-1906, public domain, Vol. 1, 179, www.jewishencyclopedia.com.

17. Taege Moberg, Marlys, *Women in League with the Lord* (St. Louis, MO: Lutheran Women's Missionary League, 2005), 14–21.

18. StoryCorps, a non-profit oral history project, has several locations as well as a portable studio where life stories can be recorded. The results are archived in the Library of Congress. For more information, see www. storycorps.net.

19. Wahlhaus, Erlene, "The Psychological Benefits of the Traditional Jewish Mourning Rituals," *European Judaism,* Vol. 38, 2005, www.jwn. org.

20. Kroeger, Catherine Clark and Mary J. Evans, *The IVP Women's Bible Commentary* (Downer's Grove, IL: InterVarsity Press, 2002), 569.

21. *Today's Light Bible,* op. cit., 1014.

22. Sadducees were enemies of the Pharisees. They accepted only the Mosaic law and denied the idea of resurrection, the existence of angels, and immortality of the soul. A high priestly group, they were influenced by the Greeks. Essenes were religious radicals who op-

posed the Temple priesthood and guarded mysterious truths that they said would govern the life of Israel when the Messiah appeared. Zealots refused to pay tribute to the Romans and led an unsuccessful revolt against them.

23. Note Jesus' criticism of the Pharisees in John 7:29–31a.

24. Romans 16:16a; 1 Corinthians 16:20; 2 Corinthians 13:12a; 1 Thessalonians 5:26 and 1 Peter 5:14a.

25. Keener, op. cit., 209.

26. More details about these studies can be found in *UnChristian, What a New Generation Really Thinks About Christianity...and Why It Matters,* by David Kinnaman and Gabe Lyons (Grand Rapids, MI: Baker Books, 2007).

27. http://www.bible-history.com/court-of-women/jewish_encyclopedia.html.

28. *LifeLight Leader's Guide,* Luke, Part 1 (St. Louis, MO: Concordia Publishing House, 1995, 2003), 35.

29. Douglas, J.D., Editor, *The New Bible Dictionary,* (Grand Rapids, MI: Wm. B. Eerdmans Publishing Co., 1962), 1336.

30. Easton, M.G., *Illustrated Bible Dictionary* (Grand Rapids, MI: Baker Book House, 1978), 445.

31. Tucker, Ruth A. and Walter L. Liefeld, *Daughters of the Church* (Grand Rapids, MI, Zondervan Publishing House, 1987), 93.

32. Ibid, 94.

33. Catholic Encyclopedia, www.newadvent.org.

34. Website of Christian Medical College, Vellore, India, www.cmch-vellore.edu.

35. For images of early surgical instruments and further information, see Part I, Chapter 3, of "The Evolution of Surgical Instruments" by John Kirkup, MD, a Fellow with the Royal College of Surgeons, on http://www.google.com/books.

36. Bloodletting is described in a complete chapter in Medicine in the Bible and the Talmud, available on books.Google.com or by doing a Google search for "bloodletting Bible times." "Nebuchadnezzar chose for himself young people without blemish (Daniel 1:4), which the Talmud says meant 'there was not even a lancet puncture on their bodies' (Sanhedrin 93b)—that is how rare it was to find a person without venesection scars (p. 151). In Sodom, if someone injured another person and he bled, the judges decided that the injured person had to pay the offender the money that the injured person saved since he no longer required venesection. (ibid)" The author, Dr. Fred Rosner, is Director of Medicine at Mt. Sinai School of Medicine, NYC, and has lectured on Jewish medical ethics in many countries. Also see www.hmc.org.qa/heartviews for an article with pictures of bloodletting equipment.

37. Catherine Clark Kroeger and Mary J. Evans, *The IVP Women's Bible Commentary,* 2002, Downer's Grove, IL, Intervarsity Press, p. 62.

38. The Pharisees liked to think of their obedience as perfect, but as Jesus pointed out, the obsessive focus on ritualistic details this required then distracted their attention from the "weightier measures of the law"—justice and mercy! See Matthew 23:32.

39. When Simon the Pharisee invited Jesus to his home, he failed to meet the customary needs of his Guest. Now Martha was being the conscientious hostess. She was doing what was expected in her role then and now, and Mary could be viewed as inconsiderate. However, because Jesus turned things upside down, because Jesus did the unexpected, the "norm" is wrong. Our standards, our cultural priorities are not His.

40. Information on foods and utensils based on the following books: Fred H. Wight, *Manners & Customs of*

Bible Lands, (Chicago, IL: Moody Press, 1953), 43-60. *The Bible Almanac,* op. cit., 465–474. Henri Daniel-Rops, translated by Patrick O'Brien, *Daily Life in the Time of Jesus,* (New York, NY: Mentor–Omega Books, 1964), 196–210.

41. Honey was a staple food. Interesting related passages include 1 Samuel 14:25–27 (Honey gave Jonathan energy when Saul foolishly forbade his troops to eat until sundown), Matthew 3:4, Luke 24:41–43 (KJV only), and Deuteronomy 32:13.

42. Evidently Lazarus died shortly after the messenger left Bethany. We can account for the body of Lazarus being in the grave four days when Jesus arrived. It took one day for the messenger to make the trip, two days of Jesus' delay and then one day for Jesus and the disciples to make the journey. Lazarus would have been buried on the day of his death.

43. Keener, op cit. p. 292.

44. See, for example, Job 4:7–9.

45. The Jews and some Christians still observe Saturday, the seventh day of the week, as a day of rest. Most Christians worship the Lord and "rest" on Sunday, the first day of the week. They regard Sunday as the "Lord's Day" because Christ rose from the dead on Sunday.

46. Yeshayahu Heiliczer, Sabbath Basics (www. teshuvah.com/articles/shabbat) and Tracey R. Rich, Judaism 101:Shabbat (www.jewfaq.org/shabbat.htm); http://www.ou.org/chagim/shabbat/thirtynine.htm.

47. Judaism 101:Shabbat, op cit.

48. Fanny Crosby information based on *131 Christians Everyone Should know,* book by editors of *Christian History Magazine,* 2000, (Nashville, TN: Christianity Today, Inc.) 160–162; Christian Biography Resources (www.wholesomewords.org/biography/bcrosby3), and www.believersweb.org.

49. American Foundation for the Blind website, (www.afb.org). The Foundation is the repository of all of Keller's papers and memorabilia.

50. Op. cit.

51. Ibid.

52. Based on biographical information on JAF website, www.joniandfriends.org.

53. Timothy M. Cook, "A Little History Worth Knowing," www.acils.com/acil/histknow.

54. For the sake of clarity, as we think of Bible "stories," we need to differentiate between the historical accounts in Scripture that record actual events and the fictional stories common whenever human beings gather for entertainment and relaxation. In the minds of many people, all "stories" are fiction. For this reason, it may be better for new believers and children if we were to talk about Bible "narratives" to emphasize the factual nature of texts commonly known as Bible "stories."

55. Keener, op. cit., 232

56. *IVP Women's Bible Commentary,* op. cit., 578.

57. Based on Bible Study #90, "The Poor Widow's Offering," from www.jesuswalk.com/lessons.

58. Taege Moberg, *Women in League with the Lord,* op. cit., 183.

59. Keener, Op. cit. 128.

60. Paul E. Kretzmann, *Popular Commentary on the Bible,* New Testament, Vol. 1 (St. Louis, MO: Concordia Publishing House, 1923), 158.

61. Easton, op. cit.,175.

62. www.templestore.com/faqs.

63. www.Americanbible.org;. ezineartarticles.com; www.futurechurch.org, and numerous other articles. In 1 Corinthians 9:1, Paul also uses his having seen the Lord as proof of his apostleship.

64. From sermon by Dr. D. William McIvor, Presbyterian Church, Sudbury, Mass., 3/25/2007, pcsudbury@pcsudburg.org.